INSTANT POT COOKBOOK
1000 DAYS INSTANT POT RECIPES PLAN

INSTANT POT COOKBOOK

INSTANT POT COOKBOOK
1000 DAYS INSTANT POT RECIPES PLAN

@ Copyright 2017 by World Good Foods Ltd   ISBN 978-1999787394
www.worldgoodfoods.com

Katie Banks

D1557961

TABLE OF CONTENTS

CHICKEN

CHILI

LAMB

||||||||||||||||||||||||||||||||||||

Port wine lamb shanks

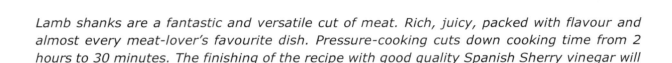

Lamb shanks are a fantastic and versatile cut of meat. Rich, juicy, packed with flavour and almost every meat-lover's favourite dish. Pressure-cooking cuts down cooking time from 2 hours to 30 minutes. The finishing of the recipe with good quality Spanish Sherry vinegar will lift the dish to a higher taste dimension.

Details

Servings: 4

Preparation time: 15 minutes

Cooking time: 40 minutes

Calories per portion: 860

Ingredients

*   4 lamb shanks, approximately 1lb. each
*   2 tbsp. olive oil
*   1 large red onion diced
*   8 – 12 cloves garlic, peeled and halved
*   1 ½ cups ruby Port wine
*   1 cup chicken or veal stock
*   1 tbsp. tomato paste
*   1 can (14oz.) chopped tomatoes
*   1 tsp. dried thyme
*   1 tsp. dried rosemary
*   3 tsp. dried parsley
*   ½ cup beef or veal stock 1 tsp. freshly ground black pepper, or to taste
*   sea salt to taste
*   1 ½ tbsp. unsalted butter
*   2 – 3 tsp. Sherry vinegar *(Vinagre de Jerez)* or aged balsamic vinegar

Preparation

1. Set the instant pot to Sauté (more/high) and add the oil. When hot brown the lamb shanks all over, one at a time. Set aside in a bowl to capture any juices.

2. Set to Sauté (less) and add the onion and garlic and cook until soft. Set to off.

3. Add the lamb juices from the bowl, Port wine, stock, tomato paste, chopped tomatoes, herbs, pepper and salt and stir to combine. Add the lamb shanks and spoon over the liquid to coat them well.

4. Place on the lid and set to manual (more/high) for 30 minutes. When done switch off and allow the pressure to release naturally. Remove the lamb shanks to a warmed serving dish and cover to keep warm.

5. Set to Sauté (more). Add the butter and vigorously whisk in until incorporated. Stir in vinegar to taste and pour the sauce over the lamb shanks.

Cooking tips

If you prefer a leaner dish you can trim off any excess fat from the lamb shanks. I particularly like the fatty richness, so I don't. Don't risk substituting Sherry vinegar with red wine vinegar; it will just not taste as good. Sherry vinegar is something you should have in the food cupboard and will once you taste it!

SOUP

||||||||||

Butternut squash soup

|||||||||||||||||||||||||||||||||||||||||||||||||||||||||||||||||||||||||||||||||||||||||||||||||||||||

A quick and easy soup recipe, irresistibly delicious when sided with slices of sour dough bread toast with melted Parmesan or cheddar cheese. Use up any left-over cooked or roasted chicken or ham by chopping into chunks and adding to the soup after the blending stage.

Details

Preparation Time: 10 min.

Cooking Time: 23 minutes

Serves: 2

Kcal per serve: 720

Ingredients

- 2 tbsp. extra virgin olive oil
- 4 ½ lb. butternut squash, peeled and cubed
- 2 white onions
- 2 diced celery stalks
- 2 carrots peeled and diced
- 5 minced garlic cloves minced
- 4 pt. chicken stock
- 2 tbsp. rosemary chopped
- 1 red chili deseeded and chopped
- ½ tsp. ground nutmeg
- ½ tsp. black pepper
- Salt to taste
- chopped chives for garnish
- ¼ cup crème fraiche or sour cream for garnish

Preparation

1. Set the instant pot to Sauté (normal) and heat the olive oil. Add the butternut, onion, celery, carrot and garlic and sauté for 3 minutes.

2. Add the chicken stock, rosemary, chili, nutmeg, black pepper and salt to taste and stir to combine. Set to manual (more/high) for 10 minutes. When done allow to depressurize naturally for 10 minutes and then release the remaining pressure. Remove the lid.

3. Puree the soup in the pot with a hand stick blender or blend, in batches, in a table top blender until smooth.

4. Taste and adjust the seasoning with salt and black pepper if desired.

5. Set to Sauté (less) and reheat the soup, stirring occasionally.

6. To serve garnish with a sprinkling of chopped chives and ½ tablespoon of crème fraiche per serving.

Cooking tips

You can easily change this recipe to be gluten free and suitable for vegetarians and vegans by substituting the chicken stock with gluten-free vegetable stock and using dairy-free yogurt in place of the crème fraiche.

Collard greens, chorizo & chicken soup

A deliciously spicy soup packed with taste and healthy such as chick peas, collard greens and tomatoes. Trim all the visible fat from the chicken thighs for a lean and healthy protein source. Serve with a drizzle of extra virgin olive oil and slices of fresh crusty bread.

Details

Preparation Time: 10 minutes

Cooking Time: 19 minutes

Serves: 4

Kcal per serve: 850

Ingredients

- 2 tbsp. olive oil
- 2 chopped medium red onions
- 6 oz. spicy Spanish chorizo, ⅛" slices
- 4 skinless & boneless chicken thighs, ½" dice
- 5 garlic cloves, chopped
- 2 pt. (4 cups) chicken stock
- 1 can (14.5oz.) diced tomatoes
- 6 oz. collard greens, de-stemmed and thinly sliced
- 3 medium red skin potatoes peeled and ½" diced
- 3 bay leaves
- 1 tsp. dried thyme
- ½ tsp. black pepper
- 1 can (16 oz.) chick peas
- salt to taste
- 2 tbsp. chopped parsley

Preparation

1. Set the instant pot to Sauté (normal) and add the oil. Add the chorizo and sauté for 1 minute. Add the onions, chicken and garlic and sauté for another 4 minutes.

2. Add the stock, tomatoes, collard greens, potatoes, bay leaves, thyme and black pepper. Stir to combine. Set to Manual (more/high) for 4 minutes. When done allow the pressure to reduce naturally for 5 minutes and then release the remaining pressure. Remove the lid.

3. Add the chick peas including the liquid and stir in. Taste the soup and adjust with salt and pepper if desired. Stir in the parsley.

4. Set to Sauté (less) and cook for 4 to 5 minutes, or until heated through and the potatoes are tender.

Cooking tips

For a lighter soup you can substitute the chorizo with chicken sausage cut into ½" chunks and use vegetable stock instead of chicken stock. If preferred use white beans such as cannellini or black-eyed beans instead of chick peas. Kale, cavolo nero or Swiss chard can be used if collard greens are not available.

Leek & potato soup

||||||||||||||||||||||||||||||||||||||||||||||||||||||||||||||||||||||||||||||||||||||||||||||||||||||||

There is nothing boring about this Vegan, gluten free soup. Serve it with chunky gluten-free croutons or toasted ciabatta. For a non-vegetarian version, you may add butter instead of olive oil and sprinkle with crisply-fried pancetta or smoked bacon.

Details

Preparation Time: 15 minutes

Cooking Time: 36 minutes

Serves: 4

Kcal per serve: 390

Ingredients

- 2 tbsp. olive oil
- 2 chopped medium white onions
- 2 chopped celery stalks,
- 2 medium carrots, peeled and chopped
- 3 minced garlic cloves
- 4 leeks (approx. 1lb.), trimmed and chopped
- 3 medium (14oz.) potatoes, peeled and diced
- 2 tbsp. chopped parsley,
- 2 vegetable bouillon cubes (vegetarian and gluten free)
- 7 ½ cups boiling water
- salt and freshly ground black pepper, to taste
- 2 tbsp. chopped chives,
- 2 tbsp. crème fraiche (optional)

Preparations

1. Set instant tot to Sauté (normal). Add the olive oil, onions, celery, carrots, garlic and leeks and sauté for 4 minutes, stirring constantly.

2. Dissolve the bouillon cubes in the water and add to the pot. Add the potatoes and parsley. Stir to combine. Set the instant Pot to Soup for 30 minutes. When done do a quick release of the pressure and remove the lid.

3. Use a hand stick blender to puree the soup in the pot until smooth. Taste the soup and adjust the seasoning with salt and pepper to taste.

4. Set to Sauté (normal) and reheat the soup.

5. Serve with a sprinkling of chives and a dollop of crème fraiche (optional).

Cooking tips

Add a fresh flavor boost to this already delicious soup by adding two tablespoons of roughly chopped leaves of fresh herbs of choice such as basil, marjoram, tarragon, thyme or cilantro when re-heating the soup.

Cream of leek and bacon soup

||||||||||||||||||||||||||||||||||||||||||||||||||||||||||||||||||||||||||||||||||||||

Get to appreciate the natural sweetness of creamed leeks with this easy to cook thick soup. The bacon provides a subtle contrasting flavour that will surely intrigue even the most sophisticated palates.

Details

Preparation Time: 10 minutes

Cooking Time: 20 minutes

Serves: 2

Kcal per serve: 570

Ingredients

- 2 Leeks, roughly chopped
- 2 Bacon strips, chopped
- 3 cups Chicken Stock
- 2 tbsp. butter
- 2 tbsp. Flour
- 1 cup Cream
- Salt, to taste
- Pepper, to taste

Preparation

1. Set pot to sauté mode.

2. Melt butter in the pot. Add chopped bacon and sauté until bacon fat is rendered off.

3. Add leeks and sauté for a minute.

4. Dust the flour into the pot and roast for a minute.

5. Stir in the chicken stock and bring to a simmer.

6. Switch to manual mode and cook on high pressure for 8 minutes. Release pressure.

7. Puree the soup with an immersion blender.

8. Stir in cream.

9. Season with salt and pepper.

Cooking tips

Go all the way and make this already excellent soup creamier and richer! Whisk an egg yolk into the cream before stirring it into the pot, then top each bowl with crisped up croutons or bacon bits... yum!

Crab and winter bamboo shoot egg drop soup

Hot, comforting, and full of flavour. This Chinese-inspired egg drop soup is simply perfect for cold winter nights and rainy days.

Details

Preparation Time: 10 minutes

Cooking Time: 10 minutes

Serves: 2

Kcal per serve: 520

Ingredients

- 1 cup Crab Meat
- 1 cup Winter Bamboo Shoots, cut into strips (alternatively artichokes)
- ¼ cup Chopped Scallions/chives
- 6 cups Chicken Broth
- 1 tablespoon, Ginger Strips
- 1 tsp. Red Chili Flakes
- 1 tablespoon Soy Sauce
- 1 tablespoon Rice Vinegar
- 1 tablespoon Sesame Oil
- 1 tablespoon Vegetable Oil
- 3 Large Eggs, beaten
- ½ teaspoon Ground White Pepper

Preparation

1. Set pot to sauté mode.

2. Heat vegetable oil and sauté scallions, ginger, chili flakes until aromatic.

3. Add crab meat and bamboo shoots. Sauté briefly.

4. Add chicken broth, soy sauce, and vinegar. Bring to a simmer.

5. Gently stir in the beaten eggs. Allow to cook for about a minute.

6. Season with salt and pepper.

7. Drizzle on sesame oil before serving.

Cooking tips

Don't overbeat the eggs to keep those streaks of egg whites distinct from the yolks. Stir in a light slurry of cornstarch and water towards the end, and you've got yourself a soup that looks like it came out of a top Asian restaurant. Don't forget the Sri Racha on the side, of course!

Instant pot chicken soup

Creamy and comforting, this healthy chicken soup will provide you with the proper nourishment to help you lose weight fast.

Details

Preparation Time: 10 min.

Cooking Time: 23 minutes

Serves: 2

Kcal per serve: 720

Preparation

1. Combine all ingredients in your instant pot, except garnishes; lock lid and cook on high pressure for 20 minutes.

2. Release pressure naturally and shred the chicken with fork. Serve in soup bowls garnished with cilantro and avocado.

Ingredients

- 1 ½ pounds chicken thighs

- 1 tsp. olive oil
- 3 cloves garlic, minced
- 1 bell pepper, thinly sliced
- 1 onion, thinly sliced
- 1 cup roasted tomatoes
- 1/2 cup water
- 2 cups bone broth
- 1/2 tsp smoked paprika

- 1 tsp oregano
- 1 tbsp. chili powder
- 1 tbsp. cumin
- 1/2 tsp sea salt
- 1/2 tsp pepper

For garnish:

- fresh cilantro
- 1 avocado

Tomato & basil cream soup

Once you try this delicious soup that is ready in less than half an hour you will never want to eat the ready-made variety again! It easily freezes so do not hesitate to cook more that you can eat! It will be handy for when you are pushed for time and fancy a quick meal: Prepare it without the cream. After defrosting add the cream and heat.

Details

Preparation Time: 12 minutes

Cooking Time: 15 minutes

Serves: 2

Kcal per serve: 770

Ingredients

- 1 tbsp. extra virgin olive oil
- 2 tbsp. butter
- 2 medium white onions chopped
- 2 medium carrots peeled and chopped
- 2 celery stalks chopped
- 4 garlic cloves crushed
- 3 ½ cups chicken stock
- 2 cans (14.5oz.) crushed tomatoes
- 1 tbsp. sun-dried tomato paste
- 1 bunch of basil/oregano roughly chopped (some leaves for garnish)
- 1 tsp. white sugar
- ½ tsp. freshly ground black pepper
- ½ tsp. sea salt
- 1 tsp. balsamic vinegar
- 1 cup Grana Padano or Parmesan cheese finely grated
- 1 cup single cream/Greek yoghourt

Preparation

1. Set the instant pot to Sauté (normal) and add the oil and butter. Add the onions, carrots and celery and sauté for 3 minutes or until the onions are softened. Add the garlic and cook for a further minute.

2. Add the stock, crushed tomatoes, tomato paste, basil, sugar, pepper and salt. Set to manual (more/high) for 5 minutes. When done allow the pressure to release naturally for 6 minutes and then release the remaining pressure. Remove the lid.

3. Use a hand stick blender to puree the soup in the pot until smooth.

4. Set to Sauté (normal) and stir in the cheese and the cream. Cook until warmed through, the cheese has melted and has been incorporated into the soup. Taste and adjust the seasoning with salt and pepper if desired.

5. Serve garnished with a basil leaf and a drizzle of extra virgin olive oil.

Cooking tips

If you have lovely ripe fresh tomatoes available, you can substitute the canned tomatoes with 3 pounds of fresh tomatoes. Peel, deseed and roughly chop the tomatoes before adding to the pot.

Instant pot roasted tomato gazpacho

A chilled savoury soup will make the perfect treat for a hot sunny afternoon. Given the highly-antioxidizing properties of tomatoes, this gazpacho will surely become the healthiest way to refresh your body way beyond the palate.

Details

Preparation Time: 2h.

Cooking Time: 10 minutes

Serves: 2

Kcal per serve: 370

Ingredients

- 8 Roma tomatoes, quartered
- 1 White onion, thinly sliced
- 1 Red bell pepper, cut into thin strips
- 2 garlic cloves, minced
- ¼ cup olive oil
- ½ tsp. sweet paprika
- ¼ tsp. red chili Flakes
- 1 tbsp. Balsamic vinegar
- Salt, to taste
- Pepper, to taste
- A handful fresh basil, for garnish

Preparation

1. Combine tomatoes, onions, bell pepper, garlic, olive oil, paprika, chili flakes, and balsamic. vinegar inside the pot. Cook on high pressure for 8-10 minutes. Release pressure.
2. Leave to cool slightly.
3. Transfer to a blender and process until smooth.
4. Season with salt and pepper.
5. Pour contents into a bowl and chill for 2 hours.
6. Garnish with fresh basil leaves and top optionally with a dollop of sour cream.

Cooking tips

Totally change the flavors in this gazpacho by simply roasting those tomatoes in the beginning. And by the way, this soup is equally amazing served hot.

Vietnamese meatball egg drop soup

Ginger, cilantro, black cardamom, mint, limes, and fish sauce come together to give this soup an authentic Vietnamese flavour. Fresh, aromatic, and light yet nourishing and totally comforting.

Details

Preparation Time: 10 minutes

Cooking Time: 15 minutes

Serves: 2

Kcal per serve: 635

Ingredients

For the Meatballs

- 1/2 lb. (225 gr) Ground Chicken
- ¼ cup Shredded Carrot
- 1 Red Chili, finely chopped
- ¼ cup chopped Green Onions
- 1 tsp. grated Ginger
- 1 tbsp. Soy Sauce
- 1 Egg
- 1 tbsp. chopped Cilantro
- 1 tbsp. chopped Mint
- ¼ tsp. Salt
- ¼ tsp. Pepper

For the Soup

- 4 cups chicken stock
- juice of 1 lime
- 1 tbsp. Fish Sauce
- 1"-piece ginger, peeled a handful Cilantro stems
- 5 pieces' black cardamom Pods
- 1 White onion, cut in half
- 1 tbsp. Sugar
- 1 Egg, beaten

Preparation

1. Combine all ingredients for the meatballs in a bowl. Mix thoroughly by hand and form into meatballs. Chill until ready to use.

2. Char the ginger and white onion on the grill or on a stove's open flame.

3. Set the pot to sauté mode.

4. Combine the chicken stock, fish sauce, lime juice, sugar, cilantro stems, cardamom pods, charred onion, and charred ginger in the pot. Bring to a simmer.

5. Switch the pot to manual.

6. Add the meatballs into the soup and cook for 15 minutes at high pressure. Release pressure

7. Season with more fish sauce and/or sugar if needed.

8. Switch to keep warm setting.

9. Stir in the beaten egg and leave on warm until ready to serve.

10. Ladle onto individual soup bowls and garnish with additional cilantro.

Cooking tips

Not much prep time available? Use chicken strips instead and save up on having to make those meatballs from scratch.

Dessert Recipes

||||||||||||||||||||||||||||||||||||||||||||||||||

All heaven gooey cake

||||||||||||||||||||||||||||||||||||||||||||||||||||||||||||||||||||||||||||||||||||||||||||||||||||||||||||||||||||||||||||||||||||||||||||||||||||

Treat yourself to the delicious combination of peanut butter and chocolate and crunchy roasted hazelnuts. Amaze your family with this incredible, delectable sticky chocolate cake. Allow the taste and scent of bananas to blend in, making this dessert not only rich but healthy.

Details

Preparation Time: 30 minutes

Cooking Time: 3 hours

Serves: 8

Kcal per serve: 590

Ingredients

- 7 oz (200 g) melted butter
- ½ cup granulated sugar
- ¾ cup vegan brown sugar
- 4 eggs, whisked (whites or whole eggs)
- 2 tablespoons peanut butter
- 2-3 tablespoons sour cream
- 2 teaspoons baking powder
- 2 tablespoons cocoa powder
- 1 cup almond flour
- ½ cup coconut flour
- 7 oz (200 g) best quality melted dark chocolate
- ¼ cup almond milk
- A few drops of vanilla essence
- 2 bananas, peeled and sliced
- 3.5 oz (100g.) roasted hazelnuts hazelnuts, crushed

Preparation

1. Grease the Instant Pot with some cooking spray.

2. Take a large mixing bowl and add the melted butter and both types of sugar into it. Blend them well using a hand/automatic blender. When the batter starts to look creamy, start adding one egg at a time and continue to whisk.

3. Add in the peanut butter, sour cream, cocoa powder and some salt. Continue to whisk for another 5-8 minutes. Thereafter, add the flour and fold it in using a spatula.
4. Pour in the melted chocolate, some milk and vanilla essence. Blend it again for 3-4 minutes (or fold using a spatula) until all the ingredients are well mixed. Be careful to not over- blend the mixture.

5. Add in the mashed bananas and crushed roasted hazelnuts. Pour the batter in the Instant Pot and spread it evenly. Cover the lid of the cooker and cook it over Slow Cooker mode in low heat for 3-4 hours.

6. Thereafter, remove the lid of the Instant Pot and insert a knife in the center to check if the cake is well-cooked.

7. Once done, remove the cake from the pot and place it on the cooling rack. Let it cool for some time. Cut it into small pieces and serve warm.

Cooking Tips

Replace almonds or walnuts for the hazelnuts to add delicious crunchiness and aroma to the cake. Drizzle a liqueur such as rum or bourbon over the cake while it warm or else put in the batter itself.

Almond barley and snow fungus pudding

||||||||||||||||||||||||||||||||||||||||||||||||||||||||||||||||||||||||||||||||||||||||||||||||||||||||||||||||

A Crock Pot based revised version of a traditional Chinese soup. Rather than relying on candied watermelon, this recipe uses cranberries and rock sugar as sweeteners. The final thicker consistency comes from using almond milk rather than water. Both almonds and Chinese barley (also known as "Job's tears") are nutritious as they come with proteins, fibre, magnesium and vitamins. It also contributes to reducing blood sugar levels.

Details

Prep Time: 20 min.

Cooking Time: 4 h. 30 min.

Serves 4

Kcal per serve: 380

Ingredients

- ½ cup of Chinese barley/ Job's tears
- 3.5 oz (100 gr) blanched almonds
- 2 cups of plain almond milk, no sugar added
- 1 cup of water
- 0.7 oz (20 gr) of white snow fungus
- ¼ cup of dried cranberries
- 1.8 oz (50gr) rock sugar
- 1 tsp. sea salt
- 2 tbsp sliced almonds, toasted

Preparation

1. Soak the snow-white fungus in water for 20 minutes. Drain and then cut into small bite-sized sections. Discard the hard stems.

2. Pulverize the blanched almonds and Chinese barley in a food processor (or the dry mill of a regular kitchen blender) to resemble coarse crumbs. Pound or crush the rock sugar into smaller pieces, not bigger than 1-inch pieces as smaller rock sugar dissolves faster in warm liquid.

3. Prepare your Instant Pot to slow cooker mode. Into the bowl, add the pulverized Chinese barley and almonds, almond milk, water, rock sugar and sea salt. You can use regular kosher salt if you like.

4. Set the pot on Low for four hours. Stir once or twice during cooking time. The Chinese barley should double in size, approximately the size of cooked beans. The milk should be thickened by the starch that is in the barley pearls.

5. After four hours, add the fungus and dried cranberries. Cook on Low for another 20-30 minutes. Stir to combine and serve in individual bowls, sprinkled with some toasted sliced almonds.

Cooking Tips

Be sure to select high-quality snow-white fungus, which is light yellow and looks fairly clean (no dark or brown spots). To get a thicker texture, include one cup of almond milk. To get a consistency more like porridge, add a half cup of water or a quarter cup of the Chinese barley.

Almond coconut rice pudding with almond milk

|||||||||||||||||||||||||||||||||||||||||||||||||||||||||||||||||||||||||||||||||||||||||||||||||||||||

This simple pudding with coconut rice and almond makes an incredible breakfast dish. It can be served either cold or hot. It tastes good as it is, or topped with healthy sprinkles, such as cranberries, avocadoes, sliced bananas, blueberries or strawberries. Shredded coconut meat, almonds and almond milk present healthy fats that reduce cholesterol and have a low caloric content.

Details

Preparation Time: 20 min

Cooking Time: 3 hours

Serves: 2

Kcal per portion: 620

Ingredients

- ½ cup of brown rice
- ½ cup of raw, shelled almonds
- 1 cup of desiccated coconuts
- 4 cups of almond milk
- 2 tablespoons of rock sugar
- 1 teaspoon of sea salt
- 1 teaspoon of ground cinnamon

Preparation

1. Rinse the ¼ cup of rice in cold water to make sure there is no hull or inedible debris left in the rice.

2. Blanch your almonds in boiling water for 2-3 minutes, drain and let cool for a while before chopping them. To cut on preparation time, simply buy a pack of blanched almonds.

3. In a food processor, pulse the blanched almonds and brown rice until they resemble coarse crumbs.

4. Set to slow cooker mode. In the bowl, add coarse crumbs of almond and rice. Then, add the desiccated coconut, almond milk, rock sugar, sea salt, and ground cinnamon. Stir to make sure all the ingredients are distributed well. Set the Instant Pot on Low for 2.5-3 hours. Stir occasionally to break any lump that may form during cooking.

Cooking tips

Allow the pudding to cool for a while in single-serve bowls. Experiment with other kinds of rice, such as wild rice or basmati. Dark brown rice and black rice (although not the sticky variety) are wonderful alternatives. Rock sugar may be replaced by other sweeteners: try honey, stevia or even brown sugar.

Cassava and sweet potatoes pudding with coconut milk sauce

||||||||||||||||||||||||||||||||||||||||||||||||||||||||||||||||||||||||||||||||||||||||||||||||||||||||||||

A pudding using sweet potatoes and fresh cassava roots, cooked slowly in dark brown sugar, allowing sweetness to soak into the roots. For extra flavour, add one teaspoon of grated ginger. To achieve a chewy, pudding-like texture, use tapioca pearls: you will not need to soak them, speeding up the making process. You may also make coconut cream sauce separately in the microwaves or the stove.

Details

Prep Time: 20 min.

Cooking time: 6 hours

Serves: 4

Kcal per serve: 480

Ingredients

- 200 grams of sweet potatoes (7.0 oz)
- 200 grams of cassava roots (7.0 oz)
- 20 grams of tapioca pearls (0.7 oz)
- 750 ml of water (more or less 3 cups) (25.36 fl oz)
- ½ cup of dark brown sugar
- ½ tsp of vanilla extract or 1 pandanus leaf
- ½ tsp. salt
- 1 cup of canned coconut cream
- ½ cup of coconut milk
- ¼ tsp. salt
- 2 tbsps. toasted sesame seeds

Preparation

1. Peel and cut young cassava root into 2-inch-thick medallions and cut each large medallion into two. If you prefer a soft-textured pudding, cut into 1-inch-thick cubes.

2. Peel and cut red or yellow sweet potatoes to 2-inch cubes. Cut into 1-inch cubes for soft-textured pudding.

3. Set slow cooker mode. Pour half the water, brown sugar or molasses, salt, vanilla extract or Pandanus leaf together in the bowl. Mix until some of the sugar has dissolved and the water changes color.

4. Add the tapioca pearls, cassava and sweet potatoes in. Add the rest of the water to cover the cassava and sweet potatoes. Set on Low and cook for 6 hours. Stir once or twice after two hours of cooking to make sure all ingredients are cooked thoroughly.

5. In the meantime, toast your sesame seeds on a non-stick sauce pan or milk pan over Medium heat until they turn light golden brown. Be careful not to toast the sesame seeds too long as they get burnt quickly over high heat.

6. Pour the coconut cream and coconut milk into the pan, along with ¼ tsp. of salt. Lower the heat and stir over low heat until the cream thickens but is not bubbly. When you see the cream starts to have bubbles on the sides, turn off the heat and let cool. You may keep the sauce in the fridge and reheat before serving.

7. After six hours, turn off your Instant Pot. Ladle the pudding into individual serving bowls and drizzle 3-4 tablespoons of coconut cream sauce on top.

Chocolate chip and cocoa pudding

Treat friends and family in a fun way by placing this delicious pudding in the center of the table and serving warm straight from the Instant Pot. For an extra layer of sweet luxury, add pitted and chopped dates to it. Try with fresh berries such as strawberries, raspberries or pitted cherries to complement the chocolate flavours.

Details

Prep Time: 15 min.
Cooking time: 2 hours
Serves: 8
Kcal per serve: 615

Ingredients

Pudding
- 1 cup light demerara sugar
- 1 cup granulated sugar
- ½ cup canola or vegetable oil
- 2 large eggs, ½ cup whole milk
- ½ cup fresh coffee, cooled
- 1 ½ tsp. almond extract
- 2 cups flour, ¾ cup cocoa powder
- 1 ½ tsp. baking soda
- 1 ½ tsp. baking powder
- ½ tsp. powdered cinnamon
- ½ tsp. salt
- ¾ cup dark chocolate chips
- ½ cup pecan nuts, chopped

Topping
- 1 cup whipping cream,
- 2 tbsp. superfine sugar
- pinch of nutmeg
- ½ tsp. vanilla extract
- cocoa powder for dusting

Preparation

1. Grease the Instant Pot with butter.

2. Whisk together the sugars, oil, eggs, coffee, milk and almond extract until well combined.

3. Sift together the flour, baking soda, baking powder, cocoa, cinnamon and salt. Add to the egg mixture and whisk until just combined. Set pot to slow cooker mode.

4. Stir in the chocolate chips and nuts until evenly spread. Pour into the Instant Pot.

5. Cover and cook on high for about 2 hours, or until a cocktail stick inserted into the center of the pudding comes out with just a few crumbs sticking to it.

6. Allow the pudding to cool, uncovered, for about 15 minutes.

7. Prepare the whipped cream topping.

Cooking tips

Dust the pudding with confectioner's sugar before topping with the whipped cream mixture. Add a little finely grated orange zest to the whipped cream to give it a citrusy lift. Replace ½ cup of all-purpose flour for 1 cup of almond flour for extra nuttiness.

Cherry cheese cake

A visually appealing, silky, smooth and creamy cheesecake. Top it with a tangy, dark cherry compote and garnish with fresh, sweet and juicy berries take it to a higher taste level. A must for all cheesecake lovers.

Details

Preparation Time: 20 minutes

Cooking Time: 50 minutes

Serves: 8

Kcal per serve: 475

Ingredients

Crust
- 1 cup Graham crackers, crumbed
- 2 tbsp. unsalted butter, melted

Filling
- 16 oz. cream cheese, softened
- ½ cup superfine sugar
- 1 tsp. vanilla extract
- ¼ cup crème fraiche or sour cream
- 1 tbsp. all-purpose flour
- 2 large free-range eggs

Cherry compote
- 2 cups (16 oz.) frozen pitted dark cherries
- ¾ cup granulated white sugar
- 2 tbsp. fresh lemon juice
- 1 tsp. lemon zest finely chopped
- ¼ tsp. vanilla or almond extract
- 2 tbsp. arrowroot starch or cornstarch

Preparation

Cherry compote

1. Add ½ the cherries, sugar, lemon juice, lemon zest and extract to the Instant Pot.

2. Set to manual (more/high) for 3 minutes. When done allow the pressure to reduce naturally for 10 minutes. Do a quick release of the remaining pressure? Remove the lid.

3. Dissolve the arrowroot starch in 2 tbsp. water. Set the Instant Pot to Sauté (normal) and gradually stir in the arrowroot until the sauce thickens.

4. Stir in the remaining cherries and add the compote to a fridge storage container with a lid. Refrigerate until needed.

Directions

1. Spray a 7" spring-form pan with non-stick cooking spray.

2. Add the crust ingredients to a mixing bowl and mix together. Press the crumbs evenly on the base and sides of the spring-form pan. Place in the freezer to firm up for 10 minutes.

3. Add the cream cheese to a mixing bowl. Using a hand mixer on medium speed gradually whisk in the sugar. Whisk in the vanilla extract, crème fraiche and flour. Whisk in the eggs one at a time until just combined. Do not over mix. Pour the mixture onto the crust.

4. Add the trivet to the Instant Pot and pour in 1 cup of water.

5. Make a sling by folding a large sheet of aluminum foil a few times. It should be long enough to go under and up the sides of the spring-form pan so that you can easily lift it out of the pot when done cooking. Make sure it doesn't affect the closing of the lid.

6. Set the instant pot to manual (more/high) for 25 minutes. When done allow the pressure to reduce naturally for 10 minutes. Do a quick release of the remaining pressure?

7. If the cheesecake is not set in the middle cook for another 3 - 5 minutes on high pressure. Note that it will firm up when refrigerated so don't over-cook.

8. Remove the cheesecake and place on a wire rack to cool. Gently dap away any water on the top of the cheesecake with some paper towel. When cool cover with cling film and refrigerate for 4 – 5 hours or overnight.

9. Remove the cherry compote from the fridge ½ hour before using. Top the cheesecake with the cherry compote and serve.

Cooking tips

Give the cheesecake more visual appeal and garnish the cherry compote with a selection of fresh berries such as sliced strawberries, blueberries or raspberries and dust with confectioner's sugar.

Key lime pie

Who doesn't crave for a deliciously creamy key lime pie? It makes a very welcome change to the usual baked-style cheesecake. Add another layer of indulgence by serving the pie with cream beaten together with honey until getting stiff peaks and finalize with a sprinkle of lime zest.

Details

Preparation Time: 20 minutes

Cooking Time: 15 minutes

Serves: 4

Kcal per serve: 350

Ingredients

Crust
- 1 cup Graham crackers, crumbed
- 3 tbsp. unsalted butter, melted
- 1 tbsp. granulated white sugar
- ¼ tsp. salt

Filling
- 4 large free-range eggs, whisked until fluffy
- ½ cup crème fraiche
- 1 can (14 oz.) sweetened condensed milk
- ½ cup fresh key lime juice
- 2 tbsp. key lime zest, finely chopped

Preparation

1. Spray a 7" spring-form pan with non-stick cooking spray.

2. Add the all crust ingredients to a mixing bowl and mix together. Press the crumbs evenly on the base and sides of the spring-form pan. Place in the freezer to firm up for 10 minutes.

3. Add the beaten eggs to a mixing bowl. Gradually whisk in the condensed milk. Gradually whisk in the key lime juice until the mixture is smooth. Add the lime zest and crème fraiche and whisk in until combined. Pour the mixture onto the pie crust. Cover the spring-form pan with a sheet of aluminum foil.

4. Add the trivet to the Instant Pot and pour in 1 cup of water.

5. Make a sling by folding a large sheet of aluminum foil a few times. It should be long enough to go under and up the sides of the spring-form pan so that you can easily lift it out of the pot when done cooking. Make sure it doesn't affect the closing of the lid.

6. Set the Instant Pot to Manual (More/High) for 15 minutes. When done allow the pressure to reduce naturally for 10 minutes. Do a quick release of the remaining pressure?

7. If the pie is still runny in the middle cook for another 3 - 5 minutes on high pressure. Note that it will firm up when refrigerated so don't over-cook.

8. Remove the pie and place on a wire rack to cool. When cool cover with cling film and refrigerate for 4 – 5 hours.

Cooking tips

Bottled key lime juice is not recommended for this recipe. If key limes are not available, you can substitute with ¼ cup fresh lemon juice and ¼ cup fresh lime juice and use the zest of regular limes for key lime zest.

Pears poached in red wine

||||||||||||||||||||||||||||||||||||||||||||||||||||||||||||||||||||||||||||||||||||||||||||||||||||||||||||||||||||||||||||

These gorgeous ruby-red pears look and taste fantastic. Just as good to be eaten warm or cold. Store them covered in the liquid and refrigerated. Try serving it with a dollop of crème fraiche or vanilla ice cream and a scattering of chopped pistachio nuts.

Details

Preparation Time: 10 minutes

Cooking Time: 3 minutes

Serves: 6

Kcal per serve: 405

Ingredients

- 1 bottle soft, fruity red wine
- 1 ½ - 2 cups sugar, to taste
- 1 stick cinnamon
- 2 cloves
- zest of ½ lemon
- zest of ½ orange
- 1 vanilla pod, split in half
- 6 medium firm ripe pears, peeled with stalk intact
- 1 – 2 tbsp. arrowroot starch dissolved in 2 tbsp. water

Preparation

1. Set the Instant Pot to Sauté (Normal). Add the wine, sugar, cinnamon, cloves, lemon zest and orange zest. Scrape the seeds from the vanilla pod and add them and the pod to the wine. Bring to a simmer and stir to dissolve the sugar. Set Instant Pot to off.

2. Peel the pears and immediately add them to the red wine mixture to stop the flesh from going brown.

3. Secure the lid and set the Instant Pot to Manual (More/High) for 3 minutes. When done do a quick release of the pressure.

4. Remove the pears from the liquid with a slotted spoon. Set aside.

5. Strain the sauce to remove the cinnamon, zest and vanilla pod and return to the pot.

6. Set the Instant Pot to Sauté (Normal). When hot gradually stir in the arrowroot starch until the sauce has thickened to your liking.

7. Pour the sauce over the pears and serve.

Cooking tips

Arrowroot starch is preferable for this recipe rather than cornstarch as it will not make the sauce go cloudy. If vanilla pods are unavailable, you can substitute it with 1 teaspoon of vanilla extract.

Rice pudding

|||||||||||||||||||||||||||||||||||||||||||||||||||||||||||||||||||||||||||||||||||||||||||||||||||||||||||||||||||||

A firm family favourite nicely served both warm or cold. Present it with a dollop of whipped cream and a scattering of blueberries and sliced strawberries or banana. Top it up by stirring in some dark chocolate chips with the golden raisins.

Details

Preparation Time: 10 minutes

Cooking Time: 32 minutes

Serves: 8

Kcal per serve: 350

Ingredients

- 1 ½ cups Arborio or Carnaroli risotto rice
- ¾ cup sugar
- ½ tsp. salt
- 5 cups whole milk
- 2 eggs
- 1 cup half and half
- 1 tbsp. maple syrup
- 1 tsp. vanilla extract
- 1 cup golden raisins (sultanas)
- pinch of nutmeg
- pinch of cinnamon

Preparation

1. Rinse the rice 3 times in cold water.

2. Add the rice, sugar, salt and milk to the Instant Pot and stir to combine. Set to Sauté (normal) and bring to the boil, stirring occasionally. When it comes to the boil secure the lid and set to manual (less/low) for 16 minutes.

3. In a mixing bowl whisk together the eggs, half and half, maple syrup and vanilla extract.

4. When the Instant Pot has completed the 16 minutes allow it to release the pressure naturally for 10 minutes and then do a quick release of the remaining pressure. Remove the lid and stir the rice mixture.

5. Stir the egg mixture into the rice. Set the Instant Pot to Sauté (normal) and bring to the boil, stirring occasionally. Switch the pot off as the rice pudding comes to the boil. Stir in the golden raisins.

6. To serve warm: pour into individual serving bowls and dust with a little nutmeg and cinnamon.

7. To chill see cooks tip. Dust with nutmeg and cinnamon when serving.

Cooking tips

If you are going to refrigerate the rice pudding, it's best to place a sheet of cling film directly onto the rice pudding. This will help stop a skin forming. If the rice pudding is too thick after refrigerating loosen it to a desired consistency by stirring in half and half or cream.

Turmeric-spiced peach compote

|||||||||||||||||||||||||||||||||||||||||||||||||||||||||||||||||||||||||||||||||||||||||||||||||||||||||||||||||||||||||||||||||||||

Fully-ripened peaches, stewed in a highly aromatic blend of turmeric, cinnamon, cloves, star anise, and black peppercorns. Preparing this compote in your Instant Pot will fill your home with aromas that are both mouth-watering and soothing.

Details

Preparation Time: 5 minutes

Cooking Time: 10 minutes

Serves: 2 Kcal per serve: 393

Ingredients

- 6 Ripe Peaches, cut in halves or sliced
- ¼ cup Maple Syrup
- 1 thumb-sized Fresh Turmeric/curry powder/ginger, cut into thin strips
- 1 stick Cinnamon
- 1 tbsp Black Peppercorns
- 6 pieces Cloves
- 4 pieces Star Anise

Preparation

1. Combine all ingredients inside the pot.
2. Cook on high pressure for 10 minutes.

Cooking Tips

Chop those peaches however you like – into halves for a perfect ala mode dessert; or into tinier chunks, for topping off yogurt, pancakes, or pretty much anything you'd serve your favorite jam with.

Instant pot carrot cardamom cake

The simple addition of ground cardamom into this recipe provides the classic carrot cake with a subtle hint of flavour and aroma that will leave your guests wondering how they had not tried it before. A gluten-free version can be made, making this recipe not only delicious but tasty.

Details

Preparation Time: 15 minutes

Cooking Time: 1 hour

Serves: 5

Kcal per serve: 500

Ingredients

- 1 cup Grated Carrots
- 1/3 cup Maple Syrup
- 1/3 cup Olive Oil
- 2 Eggs
- ¼ cup Water
- 1.5 cups Gluten-Free Baking Mix
- 1 tsp. Vanilla Extract
- 1 tsp. Baking Powder
- ½ tsp. Baking Soda
- 1 tsp. Ground Cinnamon
- 1 tsp. Ground Cardamom
- 1 tsp. Ginger Powder

Preparation

1. Whisk the following ingredients: eggs, olive oil, the vanilla extract, maple syrup, all with water within a deep bowl.

2. Whisk together gluten-free baking mix, baking powder, baking soda, ground cinnamon, ground cardamom, and ginger powder in a separate bowl.

3. Stir the dry ingredients into the wet ingredients just until fully incorporated.

4. Fold in the grated carrots until evenly distributed.

5. Transfer the batter into a lightly grease 6" round cake pan.

6. Place 2 cups of water inside the pot and set a steamer rack on top.

7. Set the filled cake pan on top of the steam rack.

8. Cook on high pressure for 40 minutes. Let pressure release naturally for 10 minutes then release remaining pressure.

9. Remove the cake pan from the pot and rest on a cooling rack before serving.

Cooking tips

Replace half of the carrots called for in the recipe with chopped pineapples for a much moister cake. Chopped nuts or dried fruit may also be folded into the batter for texture. Optionally, top the cake with your favorite cream cheese frosting for a complete treat!

Pecan nut & pumpkin pie

||||||||||||||||||||||||||||||||||||||||||||||||||||||||||||||||||||||||||||||||||||||||||||||||||||||||||||||||||||||||||

This classic pumpkin pie filling is taken to another level by adding the extra crunch and flavour of pecan nuts in the crust. Add a wow factor and decorate the pie by piping whipped cream with finely grated orange or lemon zest and a teaspoon or two of maple syrup

Details

Preparation Time: 15 minutes

Cooking Time: 35 minutes

Serves: 4

Kcal per serve: 420

Ingredients

Crust
- ½ cup (6 – 7) pecan shortbread cookies, crushed
- 2 tbsp. butter, melted
- ⅓ cup toasted pecan nuts, chopped

Filling
- 1 ½ cups (15 oz. can) pure pumpkin
- 1 ½ tsp. pumpkin pie spice blend
- ½ cup light muscovado sugar
- 1 large egg, beaten
- ½ cup evaporated milk
- ¼ tsp. salt, or to taste

Preparation

1. Spray a 7" spring-form pan with non-stick cooking spray.

2. Add the all crust ingredients to a mixing bowl and mix together. Press the crumbs evenly on the base and sides of the spring-form pan. Place in the freezer to firm up for 10 minutes.

3. Add the sugar, pumpkin pie spice blend, salt, egg and evaporated milk to a mixing bowl and whisk to combine. Add the pumpkin and whisk in. Pour the pie filling onto the pie crust. Cover the spring-form pan with a sheet of aluminum foil.

4. Add the trivet to the Instant Pot and pour in 1 cup of water.

5. Make a sling by folding a large sheet of aluminum foil a few times. It should be long enough to go under and up the sides of the spring-form pan so that you can easily lift it out of the pot when done cooking. Make sure it doesn't affect the closing of the lid.

6. Set the Instant Pot to manual (more/high) for 35 minutes. When done allow the pressure to reduce naturally for 10 minutes. Do a quick release of the remaining pressure?

7. If the pie is still not set in the middle cook for another 3 - 5 minutes on high pressure. Note that it will firm up when refrigerated so don't over-cook.

8. Remove the pie and place on a wire rack to cool. Remove the aluminum foil. When cool cover with cling film and refrigerate for 4 – 5 hours.

Cooking tips

If you can't find pecan shortbread cookies, you can substitute them with Graham Crackers or any other crisp cookie that crumbles well. Ginger Snaps cookies are a good alternative and they complement the pumpkin flavor.

Baked lemongrass and black peppercorn pineapples

||||||||||||||||||||||||||||||||||||||||||||||||||||||||||||||||||||||||||||||||||||||||||||||||||||||||||||||||||||

Sweet and savoury meet in this uniquely interesting dessert. The slight pungency of black peppercorns and citrusy fragrance of lemongrass surprisingly work with the natural sweetness of fresh pineapples. A meal-ender that truly leaves the palate fully refreshed!

Details

Preparation time: 4 minutes

Cooking Time: 4 minutes

Serves: 2

Kcal per serve: 390

Ingredients

- 1 Large Pineapple, peeled and split into 6 lengthwise wedges
- 2 tsp. Black Peppercorns, slightly crushed
- 2-3 stalks Lemongrass, bruised and bundled
- 1 tbsp. Lemon Juice
- 1 tbsp. Coconut Oil
- 2 tbsp. Honey

Preparation

1. Stir together lemon juice, coconut oil, and honey in a bowl.

2. Arrange pineapple wedges inside the pot.

3. Brush pineapples with honey-lemon mixture.

4. Sprinkle the crushed black peppercorns onto the pineapples.

5. Put bundled lemongrass into the pot and cook on low pressure for 4 minutes.

6. Serve optionally with chilled yogurt or sugar-free vanilla ice cream.

Cooking tips

Level up your presentation by dicing your pineapples into good-sized chunks and thread them into skewers made up of lemongrass stalks. Then add some chopped sweet basil or fresh mint for more vibrance and freshness.

Beef Recipes

||||||||||||||||||||||||||||||||||||||||||||||||||||||

Balsamic & rosemary roast beef

Spicy balsamic and earthy rosemary flavours will make this delicious beef roast a firm favourite. When time is not an issue a slow-cooked beef pot roast is the perfect crowning glory to a lazy day. This easy-to-prepare recipe is definitely a great choice! Serve with creamy mashed potatoes and broccoli.

Details

Preparation Time: 15 minutes

Cooking Time: 4 ½ hours

Serves: 6

Kcal per serve: 820

Ingredients

- 3 – 3 ½ lb. beef rump roast
- 1 tbsp. olive, canola or vegetable oil
- 1 large red onion, chopped
- 4 – 6 cloves garlic, crushed
- 1 – 2 tbsp. coarse ground black pepper, to taste
- 2 – 3 stalks fresh rosemary
- 2 bay leaves
- 2 tbsp. balsamic vinegar
- • 1 tsp. sherry vinegar
- • 2 tbsp. Worcestershire sauce
- 1 tbsp. dark soy sauce
- ½ cup beef or veal stock
- 1 tbsp. Dijon mustard
- 1 tbsp. muscovado or dark brown sugar
- 1 small bunch parsley, chopped

Preparation

1. Set the instant pot to Sauté (more/high) and add the oil. When hot add the beef roast and brown on all sides. Set aside the beef in a bowl.

2. Select Sauté (less), add the onions and garlic and cook until soft. Add the black pepper, rosemary and bay leaves. Switch the Instant Pot off.

3. Add the remaining ingredients, including the juices from the beef, and stir to combine.

4. Set the instant pot to slow (normal) for 4 hours. Add the beef roast, pour over the liquid mixture and secure the lid, ensuring the vent switch is set to open.

5. When done remove the beef to a warm serving dish. Remove the rosemary stalks. Taste the sauce and add salt in desired.

6. Set the instant pot to Sauté (more) and stir in the parsley. Cook for a few minutes to thicken the sauce if necessary.

Cooking tips

Give the sauce extra richness and a lovely glossy sheen by adding butter. After stirring in the parsley (step 6) add a tablespoon or two of cold butter to the sauce. Vigorously whisk in the butter until dissolved and it has been incorporated into the sauce.

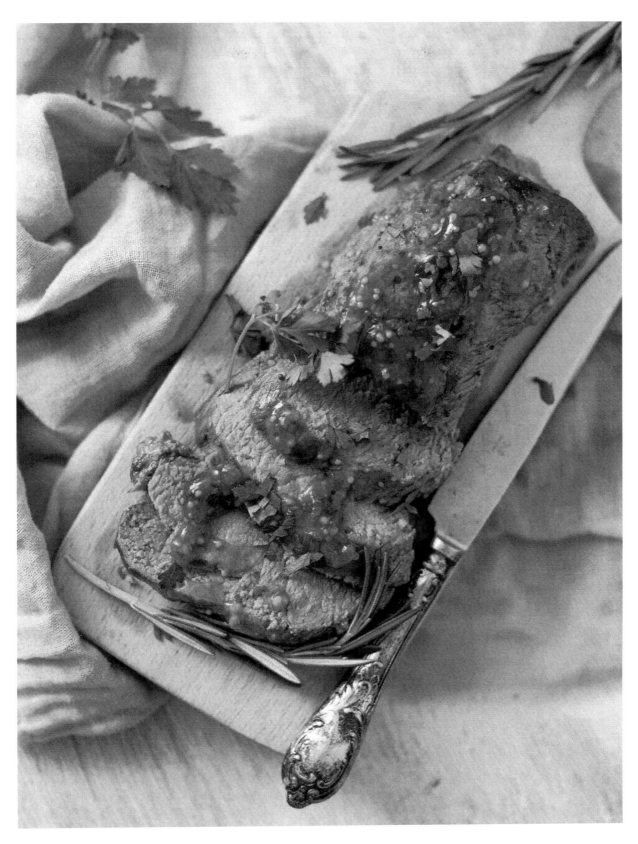

Marinara beef meatballs

This quick and easy recipe for a tasty meal takes no time at all to reach the table. Just get the pasta water on the boil when you are preparing the meatballs and drop it in the spaghetti or pasta of choice while the meatballs cook. Sprinkle over some extra Parmesan and you have a family favourite!

Details

Preparation Time: 15 minutes

Cooking Time: 20 minutes

Serves: 4

Kcal per serve: 317

Ingredients

- 1 lb. lean ground beef
- ½ red onion, finely chopped
- 2 cloves garlic, minced
- 2 eggs, beaten
- ½ tsp. red chili pepper flakes, or to taste
- ½ tsp salt
- ⅓ tsp. ground black pepper
- ½ tsp. dried basil
- ½ tsp. dried thyme
- 2 tbsp. Parmesan or Grana Padano cheese, finely grated
- 2 – 3 tbsp. olive oil
- 2 ½ cups Marinara sauce (23oz. jar) of choice
- ⅓ cup light chicken stock or water
- 3 tbsp. red wine (optional)
- 1 small bunch fresh parsley, chopped

Preparation

1. To a large mixing bowl add all the ingredients except the olive oil, Marinara sauce, chicken stock and wine. Using your hands thoroughly mix together the ingredients until evenly distributed through the ground beef.

2. Roll the ground beef mixture into balls of about 2 inches in diameter. Place them in the fridge for about 15 minutes to firm up.

3. Set the instant pot to Sauté (more/high) and add 2 tablespoons of olive oil. When hot sauté the meatballs, in batches, until browned all over. Add more oil if necessary. switch off Sauté mode.

4. Mix together the Marinara sauce, stock or water, wine (optional) and parsley. Pour a ⅓ into the pot, add the meatballs and pour over the remaining sauce.

5. Set to Manual (Normal) for 6 minutes.

6. When done allow the pressure to release naturally for 5 minutes before releasing the remaining pressure.

Cooking tips

If you use damp hands the ground beef won't be as sticky on the skin and it will be easier to roll the balls. I like using a combination of ground beef and ground pork, and even chicken, for a more interesting taste.

Spicy citrus beef

There is a touch of the Orient in this spicy, citrusy alternative to a take-away stir-fry. The preparation is easy, and the recipe is versatile and works well with other meats such as pork or lamb tenderloin, or even boneless chicken thighs. Try adding extra vegetables such as diced red bell peppers and sliced snow peas.

Details

Preparation Time: 15 minutes

Cooking Time: 25 - 30 minutes

Serves: 6

Kcal per serve: 352

Ingredients

- 2 – 2 ½ lb. flank steak, sliced into ¼ inch strips
- 2 tbsp. canola or vegetable oil
- 4 – 6 cloves garlic, finely chopped
- 1" piece fresh ginger, grated
- zest and juice of 1 lime
- zest of ½ an orange
- ¾ cup fresh orange juice
- 1 tsp. fish sauce or Worcestershire sauce
- 2 tsp. sesame oil
- 2 tbsp. soy sauce (preferably dark)
- 1 tbsp. palm sugar (or honey)
- 2 red chilli, or to taste finely sliced
- 1 tsp. red pepper flakes, or to taste
- coarse sea salt (or kosher salt) and black pepper
- 2 tbsp. cornstarch
- 8 green onions, sliced into ¼ inch lengths
- 1 small bunch cilantro, roughly chopped

Preparation

1. Season the beef slices with salt and pepper to taste.

2. Set the instant pot to Sauté (more/high) and add the oil. When hot brown the beef slices in batches so as not to overcrowd the pot. Add more oil if necessary. Set aside the beef in a bowl.

3. Select Sauté (less) and add the garlic and ginger and cook for 1 minute.

4. Add the lime and orange zest and juice, fish sauce, sesame oil, soy sauce, sugar, chili and pepper flakes. Stir to combine and scrap off all the flavorsome bits from the bottom of the pot.

5. Add the beef and the juices in the bowl and stir in. Set to Manual (more) for 12 minutes.

6. When done release the pressure and remove the lid.

7. Taste the sauce and adjust the seasoning with salt and pepper if needed.

8. Dissolve the cornstarch in a few tablespoons of water. Set the pot to Sauté (Normal) and stir in the cornstarch. Continue cooking, stirring constantly, until the sauce has thickened.

9. Stir in the half the green onions and cilantro.

10. Serve with rice and garnish with the remaining green onion and cilantro.

Cooking tips

Add an extra touch of luxury to the dish by substituting the flank steak with beef tenderloin. Cut lengthways in half and then across the grain into thin strips. If limes are unavailable, you can substitute them with lemons.

Hungarian beef goulash

This wonderfully tasty winter warmer is traditionally served as a soup but it makes a wonderful beef stew. The addition of beer gives a German twist and adds a deeper and 'hoppy' flavour to the dish. Making the paste (cooks tips) to stir in when serving is well worth the effort and a chef's 'secret' not normally found in recipes.

Details

Preparation Time: 15 minutes

Cooking Time: 45 minutes

Serves: 4

Kcal per serve: 570

Ingredients

- 2 – 2 ½ lb. beef stewing steak (chuck or round), cut into 1" cubes
- 3 – 4 tbsp. canola or olive oil
- 2 white onions, thinly sliced
- 1 green bell pepper, seeded and diced
- 4 cloves garlic, crushed
- 3 tbsp. sweet paprika
- 1 tsp. caraway seeds
- 1 tsp. sea salt
- ½ tsp black pepper
- 2 bay leaves
- 2 tbsp. tomato paste
- juice of 1 lemon
- 1 cup lager or pilsner beer (or substitute with water)
- 1 cup rich beef stock
- ½ cup sour cream, optional

Preparation

1. Season the beef cubes with salt and pepper to taste.

2. Set the instant pot to Sauté (more/high) and add the oil. When hot brown the beef cubes in batches so as not to overcrowd the pot. Add more oil if necessary. Set aside the beef in a bowl.

3. Select Sauté (less), add the onions and cook until soft. Add the bell pepper and garlic and cook for a further 2 minutes.

4. Add the paprika, caraway, salt, pepper, bay leaves, tomato paste, lemon juice, beer and beef stock and stir to combine. Add the browned beef and juices from the bowl. Stir to combine and scrap off all the flavorsome bits from the bottom of the pot.

5. Turn off Sauté and lock the lid.

6. Set the Instant Pot to Manual (more) and cook for 25 minutes.

7. Release the pressure and remove the lid. Set to Manual (Normal) and cook for a further 5 – 10 minutes to thicken the sauce.

8. Serve with a dollop of sour cream (optional).

Cooking tips

To a mortar and pestle add 2 teaspoons of caraway seeds, 4 cloves of garlic and zest of ½ a lemon and pound to form a paste. Stir in ⅓ - ½ teaspoon per portion when serving to add an extra authentic Hungarian Goulash taste boost.

Braised beef ribs

||||||||||||||||||||||||||||||||||||||||||||||||||||||||||||||||||||||||||||||||||||||||||||||||||||||||||||||||

These delicious red wine-flavored braised beef short ribs will just fall off the bone and be a real family pleaser. Serve them with a big bowl of crispy French fries and a mixed green and tomato salad or creamy mashed potatoes, butter and tarragon sauté carrots and steamed broccoli.

Details

Preparation Time: 15 minutes

Cooking Time: 1 hour

Serves: 4

Kcal per serve: 700

Ingredients

- 3 – 4 lb. beef short ribs
- sea salt and black pepper to taste
- 2 – 3 tbsp. olive or canola oil
- ½ cup (4oz.) smoked bacon lardons
- 2 medium red onions, chopped
- 4 cloves garlic, crushed
- 1 cup medium-bodied red wine
- 1 tsp. Sherry or red wine vinegar
- 2 tbsp. Worcester sauce
- ¾ cup tomato ketchup
- 1 ½ tbsp. muscovado or brown sugar
- 1 tbsp. sweet smoked paprika
- 6 stalks fresh thyme
- 2 tbsp. fresh parsley, chopped

Preparation

1. Season the ribs with salt and black pepper to taste.

2. Set the instant pot to Sauté (more/high) and add the oil. When hot brown the ribs, in batches, on all sides. Set aside the ribs in a bowl.

3. Add the bacon lardons and cook for 1 minute.

4. Select Sauté (less), add the onions and cook until soft. Add the garlic and cook for a further minute. Switch the instant pot off.

5. Add the ribs and resting juice back to the pot.

6. Add the wine, vinegar, Worcester sauce, tomato ketchup, sugar and paprika to a bowl and stir to combine. Pour over the ribs and stir to coat ribs well. Add the thyme.

7. Lock the lid with the steam vent closed. Set to manual (more/high) for 40 minutes. If the ribs are quite thick adding an extra 5 minutes.

8. When done allow the pressure to reduce for 5 minutes before releasing pressure completely.

9. Remove the ribs to a warm serving dish.

10. Stir in the parsley and pour the sauce over the ribs. If the sauce needs thickening set to Sauté (more/high) and cook for a few minutes to thicken.

Cooking tips

This recipe is also perfect with pork short ribs. Substituting the red wine with hard cider works well and imparts a wonderful apple flavor. Add ½ - 1 cup of peeled, diced apple for extra depth of flavor.

Beef and rosemary stew with stir fried vegetables

You will fall in love with this sweet and hot rosemary beef stew, made with fresh vegetables and whole spices. Adding lamb liver provides additional nutritional value and flavour. Cooked for whole 9 hours, the crunchiness of the vegetables and the pineapple's sweetness are infused throughout the entire dish.

Details

Prep + Cooking: 30min

Serves 4

Kcal per Serve: 715

Ingredients

- 2-3 cloves
- 1 tablespoon olive oil
- 17.5oz (500 gr) beef, cut into bite-size pieces
- 1 inch cinnamon stick
- 3-5 garlic cloves, peeled and cut in half
- 2 medium spring onions, chopped
- 1 large onion, sliced
- 2 medium potatoes, peeled and diced
- 2 medium carrots, diced
- 1 cup American corn
- 1 medium celery, cut into 1-inch pieces
- 1 cup lamb liver, cut in inch sized pieces
- 2 cups beef broth (or chicken stock)
- 1 cup pineapple, diced
- A few sprigs of fresh rosemary
- 2 teaspoons Worcestershire sauce
- Salt and black pepper, as per taste

Preparation

1. Turn on the Instant Pot to sauté function.

2. Pour in olive oil.

3. Add cloves, cinnamon stick, and chopped garlic. Roast until garlic turns brownish red.

4. Add the onions and potatoes and continue to fry them until onions turn slightly brown.

5. Thereafter, add the carrots, corn, and celery followed by the beef.

6. Pour in the stock, lamb liver and beef broth.

7. Sprinkle some salt, pepper, Worcestershire sauce, and pineapples.

8. Stir well.

9. Close and lock the lid then cook on high pressure for 30 minutes.

10. Release pressure naturally.

11. Drizzle lime juice before serving.

Cooking tips

Add red wine at the end and simmer the stew for another 10 minutes for some wonderful additional flavor. Let the beef marinate overnight in a mixture of thick yogurt, salt and turmeric before adding it to the pot.

Instant pot beef crock roast

The addition of avocados and roasted nuts adds some crunchiness and tasty edge to your beef roast. Marinate the meat with beer and add some corn starch followed by dropping a bunch of mixed vegetables and cheese. Let it cook slowly and savour the flavours.

Details

Level: Easy

Prep time + Cooking: 30 min

Serves: 6

Kcal per serve: 700

Ingredients

- 3 lbs. boneless shoulder chuck roast,
- Juice from half a lemon
- 1/2 cup corn starch
- 2 tablespoons olive oil
- 2 cups chopped mixed vegetables
- 2 chipotle peppers in adobo sauce, chopped
- 1 avocado, sliced
- 2 pineapple slices, roughly shopped
- 1 cube feta cheese
- 2 tbsp peanuts, roasted and crushed
- 1 cup beer (or bourbon)
- Salt and black pepper

Preparation

1. Rub some salt, pepper, and lemon juice all over the beef. Mix in the cornstarch and place it in the refrigerator for an hour.

2. Meanwhile, add some live oil into the Instant Pot, set to sauté. Add the vegetables, peppers, and avocado. Stir and cook for 5 minutes. Thereafter, add the beef, pineapples, cheese, beer, and peanuts. Sprinkle some salt and pepper as per taste.

3. Close the lid and cook on high pressure for 30 minutes. 4. Serve hot with a bread of your choice.

Cooking tips

Add pimiento-stuffed olives and raisins. Also try adding eggplant for additional flavor.

Oatmeal beef meatballs

A perfect beef meatballs recipe for beginners. Rolled oats are processed into the meal with salt and pepper and onion flakes, then combined with milk and ground beef so form the meatballs. Sear them in a no-stick pan and put them into the Instant Pot to finish cooking with the sauce.

Details

Preparation time: 15 minutes

Cooking time: 30 minutes

Serves: 4

Kcal per serving: 580

Ingredients

- 400 grams ground beef (14.0 oz)
- 3/4 cup of rolled oats
- 2 tablespoons onion flakes
- ½ cup of milk
- 1 egg
- A pinch of salt and pepper to taste
- 2 tablespoons coconut oil

Sauce
- 1 tablespoon brown sugar
- 1/2 cup tomato sauce
- 1/2 cup chopped crushed tomatoes
- 1 cup of beef broth
- 1/4 cup hickory smoke barbecue sauce
- ½ tsp salt
- ½ tsp freshly ground black pepper

Preparation

1. In a food processor, blend the rolled oats, onion flakes, salt and pepper. Process until the oat resembles a coarse meal. Set aside.

2. In a bowl, whisk the milk and the egg. Break up the ground beef with your fingers. Add the ground beef to the egg and milk mixture. Mix well. Then, add the oatmeal. Add more milk if the mixture is too dry. Form the beef mixture into 1-inch balls or approximately the size of a golf ball.

3. Make the sauce. In a bowl, whisk the brown sugar, tomato sauce, crushed tomatoes, hickory smoke barbecue sauce, beef broth, salt, and pepper.

4. In the Instant Pot set to sauté, heat 2 tablespoons of coconut oil. You may us olive oil, but personally, I prefer coconut oil because our body processes and turns coconut oil into energy faster than other vegetable oil.

5. Once the oil is hot, sear the meatballs, turning them occasionally to prevent burning, until the outer part forms golden brown crusts.

6. Add the sauce into the pot.

7. Close the lid and cook on low pressure for 30 minutes.

8. Let the pressure out via quick release.

9. Serve the meatball on top of a mashed potato, baked potato, boiled pasta or steamed vegetables.

Cooking tips

Make the meatballs with other types of ground meat, such as turkey or chicken. White meat is waterier, so consider reducing the amount of liquid you use.

South east Asian beef ribs and white radish stew

A wonderful beef stew including root vegetables. As a very clear soup it makes an excellent slow cooking choice. Get the meat by cooking the ribs in the pot overnight and then finish them the next morning, or else you can prepare the root vegetables at night and then finish them in the Instant Pot the following morning.

Details

Prep Time: 15-20 minutes

Cooking Time: 30 minutes

Serves: 2

Kcal per serve: 650

Ingredients

- 7 oz (200 gr) of beef loin, cut into 1 or 2 inch cubes
- 1 cup of Portobello mushroom, washed, gills and stems removed, and cut into 1-inch cubes
- 1 cup of peeled and cubed potatoes (use hard potatoes)
- 1 cup of carrots, cut into 1-inch cubes
- 1 cup of onions, cut into 1-inch chunks
- 1 cup of cherry tomatoes, cut in half
- 1 cup of tomato puree
- 2 cups of beef stock
- 2 tbsps. all-purpose flour
- 2 bay leaves
- 1 tsp. dried rosemary
- 1 tsp. of cayenne pepper powder
- salt and ground black pepper
- 2 tbsps. chopped parsley leaves
- 2 tbsp. olive oil

Preparation

1. Cut the short ribs into sections. Cutting into sections allows you to bite it easily when the stew is done. If the ribs are bought from the butcher, you may ask him or her to cut the ribs for you.

2. Set the Instant Pot to sauté and heat the coconut oil.

3. Season the short ribs with salt and pepper.

4. Add the short ribs into the pot and sear until brown.

5. Add the radish, celery, ginger, shallots, and garlic into the pot. Sauté until fragrant.

6. Add the stock and stalk of lemongrass.

7. Cook on high pressure for 30 minutes.

8. Let the pressure release naturally.

9. Season with salt and pepper as needed.

Cooking tips

Ribs usually need a rather long time for cooking. If you enjoy a chewy texture, cook them on high pressure for 30 minutes. Add 10-15 minutes of cooking time if you prefer falling-off-the-bone doneness.

Classic beef stew with mushroom and peas

|||||||||||||||||||||||||||||||||||||||||||||||||||||||||||||||||||||||||||||||||||||||||||||||||||||||||||||

A classic stew beef recipe, adding Portobello mushrooms for an interesting twist. The mushrooms provide an exotic flavour and a meaty, chewy texture. Remove the gills with a spoon and slice the outer edge so it can be sliced into small cubes.

Details

Prep Time: 20-30 minutes

Cooking Time: 30 minutes

Serves: 2Kcal per serve: 640

Ingredients

- 7 oz (200 gr) of beef loin, cut into 1 or 2 inch cubes
- 1 cup of Portobello mushrooms, washed, gills and stems removed, and cut into 1-inch cubes
- 1 cup of peeled and cubed potatoes (use hard potatoes)
- 1 cup of carrots, cut into 1-inch cubes
- 1 cup of onions, cut into 1-inch chunks
- 1 cup of cherry tomatoes, cut in half
- 1 cup of tomato puree
- 2 cups of beef stock
- 2 tbsps. all-purpose flour
- 2 bay leaves
- 1 tsp. dried rosemary
- 1 tsp. of cayenne pepper powder
- salt and ground black pepper
- 2 tbsps. chopped parsley leaves
- 2 tbsp. olive oil

Preparation

1. Season the beef loin with salt and pepper, then dredge in flour.

2. Set the Instant Pot to sauté and heat olive oil.

3. Add the beef and sear until brown on all sides.

4. Add the carrots and onions. Sweat until onions are translucent.

5. Add tomato puree and roast for 1-2 minutes.

6. Add the cherry tomatoes and roast briefly in the pot.

7. Add the stock, bay leaves, rosemary, and cayenne pepper.

8. Close the lid and cook on high pressure for 30 minutes.

9. Let the pressure release naturally.

10. Season with salt and pepper if needed.

11. Garnish with fresh parsley before serving.

Spinach Ndole

The nutty creaminess of roasted peanuts, the richness of natural beef broth and the distinct briny flavour of smoked cod effectively come together, giving this native African dish seriously complex flavours. Hearty and flavourful... indeed a perfect one pot wonder

Details

Preparation Time: 5 minutes

Cooking Time: 5 minutes

Serves: 4

Kcal per serve: 830

Ingredients

- 1.75 lb (750gr) Spinach Leaves
- 1/2lb. (225 gr) Ground Beef
- 1/4 lb. (110 gr) Smoked Cod, flaked
- 3/4 lb. (350 gr.) Roasted Peanuts
- 2 stalks Leeks, roughly chopped
- 2 White Onions, thinly sliced
- 6 cloves Garlic, minced
- 2 cups Beef Stock
- Salt, to taste
- Pepper, to taste

Preparation

1. Combine peanuts, leeks, onions, garlic, and beef stock in a blender. Pulse until smooth.

2. Put spinach leaves, ground beef, smoked cod, and peanut mixture inside the pot.

3. Cook on high pressure for 5 minutes. Release pressure.

4. Season with salt and pepper.

Cooking Tips

For a deeper-flavored and heartier Ndole, cuts of beef rib may be used instead of ground meat, adjusting stewing times accordingly. Topping the dish with sautéed shrimps may also be worth considering for a version that's closer to the authentic.

Chicken Recipes

||||||||||||||||||||||||||||||||||||||||||||||||||||||||||

Chicken Santa Fe style

A tasty and healthy shredded chicken and beans dish taking no time at all to prepare. Serve it with rice or corn tortilla chips. Add extra flavour by garnishing with a drizzle of hot sauce and a sprinkling of fresh cilantro, chopped green onions and shredded cheese.

Details

Preparation time: 10 min.

Cooking time: 15 minutes

Serves: 4

Kcal per serve: 510

Ingredients

- 24 oz. skinless chicken breasts
- 1 ½ cups chicken stock
- 1 can (14.5oz.) diced tomatoes
- 1 can (15oz.) black beans, drained
- 1 cup frozen corn
- 4 green onions, chopped
- 1 green chili pepper, chopped
- 1 tsp. powdered onion
- 1 tsp. powdered garlic
- 1 tsp powdered cumin
- 1 tsp. cayenne pepper, or to taste
- ¼ tsp. black pepper
- Salt to taste
- 4 tbsp. chopped cilantro

Preparation

1. Season the chicken breasts with salt and black pepper to taste.

2. Add all the remaining ingredients to the pot and stir to combine.

3. Lay the chicken breasts on top and gently push them down into the liquid. Secure the lid ensuring the steam vent is closed.

4. Set the Instant Pot to Manual (Normal) and set the time for 10 minutes. When done allow the pressure to reduce naturally for 5 minutes before releasing the remaining pressure and removing the lid.

5. Take the chicken breasts out of the pot and shred using 2 forks. Return the shredded chicken to the pot and stir the shredded chicken into the sauce.

Cooking Tips

You can substitute the chicken breasts with fresh turkey breast. Quarter the turkey breast to allow the flavors to penetrate. This recipe also works well with skinless, boneless chicken thighs for only a small increase in calories.

Chicken, butternut & apple stew

Running late? why not trying this super easy, low fat, low calorie chicken stew? It will be on the table in less than half an hour! Skinless and boneless chicken thighs or turkey breast work just as well as chicken breasts for this recipe. Boost the apple flavour by splitting 1/2 stock and 1/2 cider.

Details

Preparation Time: 10 minutes

Cooking Time: 12 minutes

Serves: 4

Kcal per serve: 400

Ingredients

- 4 x 1lb. skinless, boneless chicken breasts
- 1 tbsp. olive oil
- salt and black pepper, to taste
- 1 medium sweet potato, peeled and cubed
- 5 cups (approx. 2lb.) butternut squash, peeled and cubed
- 1 granny smith apple, peeled and diced
- 1 medium onion, diced
- 3 cloves garlic, minced
- ¼ tsp. kosher salt
- ¼ tsp. black pepper
- 1 cup chicken stock
- 5 tbsp. fresh basil, chopped
- 5 tbsp. fresh parsley, chopped
- 2 bay leaves

Preparation

1. Season the chicken breasts with salt and pepper to taste. Set the Instant Pot to Sauté (More/High), add the oil and when hot sauté the chicken breasts for a minute on each side to brown.

2. Add all the remaining ingredients to the Instant Pot, stir to combine and secure the lid with the steam vent off. Select Manual (More/High) or Poultry and set for 10 minutes.

3. When done allow the pressure to release naturally for 5 minutes before doing a quick release of the remaining pressure. Remove the lid.

4. Taste and adjust the seasoning with salt and pepper if desired.

Cooking tips

Butternut squash has a tough skin that can be really difficult to peel. Here is a great tip to make the task easier. Slice the top and bottom off the butternut. Microwave it for 3 – 5 minutes. Allow to cool and peel. Simple!

Garlic & lime chicken

The sweet and smoky honey-paprika flavours, lifted by zesty lime, blend deliciously with the earthiness of the garlic. You will be planning the next mouth-watering Garlic and Lime Chicken meal before you finish this one. Garlic-lovers might even add a few extra cloves to the recipe!

Details

Preparation Time: 10 minutes

Cooking Time: 20 minutes

Serves: 4

Kcal per serve: 540

Ingredients

- 4 chicken hind quarters (leg & thigh)
- salt and black pepper, to taste
- 1 tbsp. coconut or olive oil
- zest of 1 lime
- 1 tbsp. lime juice
- 2 tbsp. honey
- 1 tsp. palm sugar (optional)
- 6 cloves garlic, thinly sliced
- 1 red chili, finely sliced
- ½ cup chicken stock
- 2 tbsp. cilantro, chopped
- 1 tsp. dried thyme
- ½ tsp. black pepper
- 2 tsp. smoked picante paprika
- 1 tsp. ground allspice
- 4 green onions, shredded
- extra virgin olive oil

Preparation

1. Season the chicken with salt and pepper.

2. Set the instant pot to Sauté (More/High) and add the oil. When hot sauté the chicken legs one at a time until browned all over. Set aside in a bowl.

3. Add the lime zest and juice, honey, sugar (optional), garlic, chili, stock, herbs and spices to the pot and stir to combine. Add the chicken and any resting juices and coat well with the mixture.

4. Set the instant pot to manual (more/high) for 15 minutes. When done allow the pressure to release naturally for 5 minutes. Quick release any remaining pressure.

5. Serve garnished with shredded green onions and a drizzle of olive oil.

Cooking Tips

If you don't have allspice you can substitute it with ½ teaspoon ground cinnamon, ¼ teaspoon ground cloves and a ¼ teaspoon ground nutmeg. Use fresh thyme if available. Use 3 teaspoon thyme leaves for 1 teaspoon of dried.

Honey, mustard & lemon chicken

This quick and easy recipe is a great alternative to regular old grilled or fried chicken. The lemon and honey are wonderfully complemented by the earthy mustard and herb scents. Try using a combination of lemon and lime for extra citrus zing. If preferred, use thighs only with bone-in or de-boned.

Details

Preparation Time: 10 min.

Cooking Time: 10 minutes

Serves: 4

Kcal per serve: 525

Ingredients

- 2 – 2 ½ lb. free range chicken pieces (4 thighs & 4 drumsticks)
- salt and black pepper
- 1 ½ lb. redskin potatoes, quartered
- 3 tbsp. olive oil
- zest and juice of 1 lemon
- 2 tbsp. honey
- ¾ cup chicken stock
- 2 tbsp. Dijon mustard
- 2 garlic cloves, crushed
- 2 tbsp. rosemary, chopped
- 2 tbsp. thyme, chopped
- 2 tbsp. oregano, chopped

Preparation

1. Season the chicken pieces with salt and black pepper to taste and add to the Instant Pot.

2. Add the quartered potatoes.

3. In a bowl mix together the olive oil, lemon zest and juice, honey, chicken stock, mustard, garlic and herbs. Pour over the chicken and potatoes and stir to combine.

4. Cook on MANUAL for 15 minutes. Quick release the pressure when done.

5. Taste and adjust the seasoning with salt and pepper if desired.

Cooking tips

If fresh herbs are unavailable, you can substitute them with two tablespoons of Italian dried herb seasoning. Chicken with the skin on will give extra flavor to the dish but it can be removed to lower the calories.

Maple & sesame chicken

This is a real crowd-pleaser of a dish and is bound to become a regular in your menu. The crunchy toasted sesame seeds add a delicious nuttiness to the sweet and sticky chunks of tender chicken breast. Serve with fragrant jasmine rice and steamed green vegetables such as broccoli and snow peas.

Details

Preparation Time: 10 minutes

Cooking Time: 10 minutes

Serves: 4

Kcal per serve: 560

Ingredients

- 2 lbs. skinless chicken breast, 1 ½" dice
- salt and black pepper, to taste
- 2 tbsp. canola or peanut oil
- 1 medium onion, finely diced
- 3 cloves garlic, minced
- 1 tsp. fresh ginger, grated
- zest of 1 small lemon, finely sliced
- 1 tsp. lemon juice
- ⅓ cup soy sauce (preferably low sodium)
- ¼ cup tomato ketchup
- ⅓ cup maple syrup
- 2 tsp. sesame oil
- ¼ tsp. black pepper
- ½ tsp. chili flakes, or to taste
- 2 tbsp. white sesame seeds, toasted
- 4 green onions, sliced (reserve some for garnish)
- 1/2 small bunch cilantro, chopped (reserve some for garnish)

Preparation

1. Season the chicken with salt and pepper.

2. Set the Instant Pot to Sauté (More/High) and add the oil. When hot sauté the chicken pieces, in batches, until browned all over. Set aside in a bowl.

3. Set to Sauté (Normal) and add the onion, garlic and ginger. Sauté for 3 minutes until the onions are soft.

4. Add the lemon zest and juice, soy sauce, ketchup, maple syrup, sesame oil, pepper and chili flakes. Add the chicken and any resting juices. Set to Manual (More/High) for 3 minutes. When done do a quick pressure release. Remove the lid.

5. Add the green onions and cilantro and stir in.

6. To serve sprinkle with sesame seeds, green onions and cilantro.

Cooking tips

If maple syrup is unavailable or you prefer the taste you can substitute it with honey. If the sauce is a bit runny dissolve 2 – 3 tablespoons of cornstarch in water. Set to Sauté (Normal) and slowly add the cornstarch, stirring constantly, until you have the desired thickness.

Chicken tandoori

These juicy, tender chicken drumsticks and thighs will get your taste buds tingling and are packed of spicy and fragrant Indian flavours. Perfect accompaniments are fluffy Basmati rice and warm naan breads. For extra depth of flavour, marinate the chicken by covering it in the fridge for a few hours or even leaving it overnight.

Details

Preparation Time: 15 minutes

Cooking Time: 18 - 21 minutes

Serves: 2

Kcal per serve: 710

Ingredients

- 12 free-range chicken drumsticks & thighs (approx. 3.3 lbs.)
- 2 tbsp. cilantro leaves
- 4 green onions, sliced
- 1 green chili, thinly sliced

Sauce
- 1 medium onion, chopped
- 4 cloves garlic, chopped
- 1 tbsp. fresh ginger, grated
- 2 red chili peppers, or to taste
- 2 tbsp. fresh lemon juice
- 1 tsp. ground cumin
- 1 tsp. ground coriander
- 1 tsp. turmeric
- 1 tbsp. paprika
- 1 tbsp. garam masala
- 1 tsp. black pepper
- 1 tsp. coarse sea salt, or to taste
- 1 cup plain yogurt
- ¼ cup chicken stock
- ½ small bunch cilantro, chopped

Preparation

1. Remove the skin from the chicken drumsticks and thighs. Add to a large bowl.

2. Add all the Paste ingredients to a blender except the chicken stock. Process the ingredients gradually adding enough stock until you have a smooth thick paste. If necessary, add more liquid.

3. Add the paste to the chicken and coat them well.

4. Set the Instant Pot to Manual (More/High) for 18 minutes and add the chicken. When done do a quick release of the pressure.

5. Remove the chicken and sauce to a large baking tray, spreading the chicken pieces in one layer.

6. If the sauce is too runny remove the chicken pieces to a baking tray. Set to Sauté (More/High) and simmer the sauce until you have the desired thickness. Pour over the chicken pieces and turn chicken pieces to coat them well.

7. Pre-heat your broiler to high and broil the chicken on both sides until nicely browned. Keep your eye on the chicken as the sauce will burn easily.

8. Remove to a warm serving dish and garnish with cilantro leaves, sliced green onions and sliced chili.

Cooking tips

You can substitute the garam masala powder with a tablespoon of garam masala paste. If garam masala is not available, you can substitute with a tablespoon of medium curry powder. It will taste a little different but just as good.

Instant pot roasted tandoori chicken

Perfectly succulent roasted chicken thighs flavoured in a spiced yogurt mix, then finished off to crisp on a hot grill. Serve this Indian classic for an alternative twist to your usual Sunday BBQ.

Details

Preparation Time: 8 hours

Cooking Time: 15 minutes

Serves: 4

Kcal per serve: 690

Ingredients

- 6 Pieces Chicken Thighs, bone-in
- ½ cup Plain Yogurt
- 1-2 tbsp. Tandoori Paste
- 1 tbsp. Lemon Juice
- Salt, to taste
- Black Pepper, to taste

Preparation

1. Mix yogurt, lemon juice, and tandoori paste in a large bowl.

2. Toss the chicken thighs into the tandoori mixture and marinate overnight.

3. Season the chicken with salt and pepper.

4. Put the chicken, marinade, and half cup of water into the pot. Cook on high pressure for 10 minutes. Release pressure.

5. Take the chicken thighs out of the Instant Pot and sear for 3 minutes per side on the grill.

Cooking tips

For a more spiced up tandoori, adjust the chili paste to your preference, then cool things down with a quick raita of yogurt, cucumbers, and chopped mint leaves on the side.

Chicken Shawarma with Spicy Orange Sauce

|||||||||||||||||||||||||||||||||||||||||||||||||||||||||||||||||||||||||||||||||||||||||||||||||||||||||||||||||||||||||||||||||||||||||||||||

Nothing spells out healthy more than a serving of chicken thighs and breasts cooked in coconut oil. Savor each bite of our nutrient rich low carb chicken recipe that will take you a few steps closer to your ideal weight.

Details

Prep Time: 10 minutes

Cooking Time: 15 minutes

Serves: 4

Kcal per serve: 560

Ingredients

- 3/4 pound chicken thighs
- 3/4 pound chicken breasts, sliced
- coconut oil
- 1/8 tsp. cinnamon
- 1/4 tsp. chili powder
- 1 tsp. ground cumin
- 1/4 tsp. ground allspice
- 1/4 tsp. granulated garlic
- 1/2 tsp. turmeric
- 1 tsp. paprika
- 1 cup water, ½ cup orange juice
- 1/2 cup chicken broth
- 1 tbs. hot chili sauce
- 4 tbsp. tomato paste
- ½ cup fresh orange juice
- 1 tbsp. chopped chives
- 1/3 cup fresh lemon juice
- 2 tbsp. grated ginger

Preparation

1. Mix all ingredients in your instant pot and lock lid; cook on poultry setting for 15 minutes and then release pressure naturally.
2. Serve chicken with sauce over mashed sweet potato drizzled with tahini sauce.
3. Make the sauce: add a teaspoon of olive oil to a skillet and set over medium high heat; sauté grated ginger for 1 minute and then stir in the remaining ingredients, except, hot chili sauce and lemon juice. Cook until thick and then stir in chili sauce and lemon juice.
4. Serve chicken with sauce.

Cooking tips

Use chicken thighs instead of breasts with same cooking time. You can substitute coconut oil for olive oil in this recipe.

Chicken adobo with orange salsa

Inspired by the traditional Filipino chicken adobo. To make a satisfying main dish, try serving it with some steamed rice and orange salsa. Buy salsa from the store, and have a butcher cut your chicken breast to make this recipe even easier to make. Simply chop all the ingredients per the directions, mix the salsa and then put it all into the Instant Pot with the chicken.

Details

Prep Time: 25-30 minutes

Cooking Time: 10 minutes

Serves: 2

Kcal per serve: 823

Ingredients

- 17.5 oz (500 gr) chicken breast
- ½ cup of soy sauce
- 1.5 tablespoons garlic (2-3 cloves)
- 2 tablespoons white vinegar
- ¼ cup of chicken broth
- 1 teaspoon ground black pepper
- 2 bay leaves
- 2 tablespoons honey

Salsa
- 1 and ½ cup of fresh tomato, chopped
- ½ cup oz shallots, chopped
- 2 fresh jalapeño, chopped
- ½ cup of orange sections
- juice of half a lime
- ½ cup chopped cilantro
- salt and pepper to taste

Preparation

1. Prepare the salsa first. Wash and chop the tomatoes (2-3 tomatoes will do). Keep the seeds if you prefer sour salsa. Remove them if you prefer a sweeter one. Chop the shallots. Cut the orange sections into two or three parts each. Press the lime to get 1-2 tablespoons of juice. Remove the stem and seeds of the jalapeño peppers. Rinse the fresh cilantro under running tap water and chop them well to get half a cup of cilantro.

2. In a small bowl, mix all the salsa ingredients together, sprinkle with salt and pepper to taste. Keep the bowl in the fridge, covered until you are ready to eat.

3. Prepare the chicken. Cut the chicken breast to 2-inch cubes. Set aside. Then, peel and crush the garlic. Mince them finely to get 2 tablespoons of garlic. To save time, you may use a garlic press and press the garlic well.

4. In a bowl, mix the soy sauce, garlic, white vinegar, chicken broth, ground black pepper, and honey. Stir until all ingredients are well blended.

5. Combine the chicken breasts and soy sauce mixture in the Instant Pot and cook on high for 10 minutes.

6. Let the pressure release naturally.

7. Serve adobo with a bowl of steamed rice and a side of orange salsa.

Cooking tips

Dutch oven cooking: Arrange the chicken breast cubes into the oven, and then pour the Adobo sauce over it, stirring to coat. Cover and bake for two hours in a preheated oven.

Stuffed chicken breast

Revolutionize the menu with a stuffed whole chicken packed with mixed herbs, mushrooms and olives. With a sauce made with delicious vegetables and a hung curd chicken filled with chicken mince you will impress any friends or invites. Show it off on your party platter, your guests will want to dig right in!

Details

Prep Time: 15-20 minutes

Cooking Time: 10 minutes

Serves: 8

Kcal per serve: 750

Ingredients

- 500 grams chicken mince (17.6 oz)
- 2 tablespoons black olives, chopped
- 6-8 green olives, chopped
- 6-8 button mushrooms, sliced
- salt and freshly ground black pepper
- 2 teaspoons mixed herbs(oregano, thyme, basil, Italian seasoning)
- 2 teaspoons paprika
- 2 tablespoons olive oil
- 1 tsp turmeric
- 2 teaspoons soy sauce
- 1 tsp vinegar
- 2 onions, chopped
- 5 garlic cloves, chopped

Sauté chicken
- 4-5 pound whole chicken
- 1 cup sliced onion
- 1 cauliflower, cut into florets
- 4 to 5 carrots, diced
- 2 capsicums, diced
- 1 cup hung curd
- juice of one lemon
- 1.5 cups chicken stoc

Preparation

1. Take a non-stick pan and add the chopped onions and garlic. Fry until the onions caramelize and turn dark brown in color. Remove from the heat and keep aside.

2. While the onions cool, take a large mixing bowl and add the chicken mince, along with all the other ingredients for the filling. Add in the caramelized onions and mix it well.

3. Rinse the whole chicken with water and pat dry with paper towels. Stuff the cavity of the chicken with the prepared chicken mince mix. Keep aside.

4. Meanwhile, pour some oil into the Instant Pot set to sauté. Add the sliced onions, cauliflowers, carrots, and capsicums. Sauté briefly.

5. Put in the hung curd and place the whole chicken inside. Sprinkle some salt and pepper and mix it well. Try to mix and spread the curd all over the chicken.

6. Add the chicken stock.

7. Cover and cook on high for 10 minutes.

8. Release the pressure naturally.

9. Once done, sprinkle some lemon juice on top and place the chicken in a serving dish. Serve hot.

Cooking tips

Add some Balsamic vinegar for additional flavour. Use mint leaves and chopped coriander either in the mince stuffing or as a garnish.

Spicy five peppers hot chicken wings

A very hot chicken wings, certainly not indicated for the squeamish. Rather than utilizing grocery store hot sauce, this recipe requires your own making of the sauce. All it requires is putting all the sauce's ingredients in a blender or food processor and then pouring them in the Instant Pot. Perfect for movie nights, football games, or impressing guests.

Details

Prep Time: 15-25 minutes
Cooking Time: 10 minutes
Serves: 4
Kcal per serve: 790

Ingredients

- 400 grams of chicken wings (6 pieces) (14.0 oz)
- ¼ cup of all-purpose flour
- 3 cups of coconut oil for frying
- 3 cloves garlic
- ¼ cup of chopped onions
- 1 cup of fresh cayenne peppers
- ½ cup of jalapeño peppers
- 1 tbsp. smoked paprika powder
- 1 tsp. Szechuan peppercorn powder
- 1 tbsp. dried bird's eye chilies
- 1 medium-sized tomato, chopped
- ½ tbsp. of coconut oil
- ½ cup of chicken broth
- 3 tsp. brown sugar
- 1 tsp. lime zest
- 1 tbsp. lime juice
- salt and pepper to taste

Preparation

1. Take a bowl and add the flour with a pinch of salt and pepper. Mix well. Add the chicken wings. Coat well.

2. Prepare to deep fry the chicken wings. Heat a non-stick pan over medium high heat. Pour the 3 cups of coconut oil to coat at least 1-inch from the bottom of the pan. Wait until small bubbles appear. Deep fry the coated chicken wings. Set aside. Pat some of the oil with kitchen towel. Alternatively, you may bake or pan-sear the chicken wings. Coat in flour and bake in a preheated 350ºF oven for 15-20 minutes or until the wings change color completely. You shouldn't see any pink parts.

3. Prepare a blender. You can use an immersion blender or a food processor. Blend together the garlic, onions, cayenne peppers, jalapeño, bird's eye chilies, brown sugar, paprika powder, Sichuan peppercorn powder, chicken broth, lime zest and lime juice, chopped tomato. If the mixture is too thick, add more chicken broth. The sauce should not be too thick and not runny.

4. Simmer the sauce for 10-15 minutes in the Instant Pot.

5. Add the chicken wings and coat evenly in the sauce.

6. Close the lid and cook on low pressure for 5 minutes.

7. Let the pressure out via quick release.

Cooking Tips

If you don't have allspice you can substitute it with ½ teaspoon ground cinnamon, ¼ teaspoon ground cloves and a ¼ teaspoon ground nutmeg. Use fresh thyme if available. Use 3 teaspoon thyme leaves for 1 teaspoon of dried.

Sweet and spicy soy roast chicken

A tantalizing mixture of spicy, sweet and hot: the ultimate spicy chicken recipe. The chicken is roasted primarily over a medium-hot flame, along with carom seeds to get that smoky aroma and flavour. Then the chicken is slow cooked in vegetables and wine.

Details

Prep time + cooking: 30 minutes

Serves: 2

Kcal per serve: 600

Ingredients

- 2 tablespoons olive oil
- 1 teaspoon carom seeds
- 1 full chicken breast
- 1 medium-sized onion. Sliced
- 8-10 garlic cloves, minced
- 1 eggplant, cut in cubes
- 1 capsicum, diced
- 9oz (250gr) Pumpkin, cut into cubes
- 1 habanero pepper, diced
- 2 tomatoes, steam, grinded
- 1 cup dry red wine
- 2-3 tablespoons soy sauce
- 2 cups chicken broth
- 2 teaspoons oregano, dried

Preparation

1. Set the instant pot to sauté.

2. Heat olive oil then add the carom seeds. As they start to temper, add the chicken breasts and sear until brown on both sides. Remove from the pot and set aside, draining any excess oil.

3. In the same pot, add the onions and garlic. Cook until the garlic looks reddish brown.

4. Thereafter, add the eggplant, capsicum, and pumpkin. Stir and mix them well while adding the peppers. Stir in the pureed tomatoes.

5. Stir in the wine, soy sauce, and chicken broth.

6. Add the chicken.

7. Sprinkle salt, pepper, and dried oregano.

8. Pour in chicken broth.

9. Close the lid and cook on high pressure for 10 minutes.

10. Let the pressure release naturally.

11. Serve hot with your choice of bread.

Cooking tips

Give this recipe a tangy taste by adding vinegar. Also consider substituting thick and sour yogurt for the red wine. It will provide additional texture and thus make the chicken more aromatic and softer.

Sweet and spicy three cups chicken

"Three Cups" or "San Bei Ji" chicken is one of the simplest Asian chicken dishes but it still will amaze your guests. "Three Cups" is the estimated total of seasonings used in the recipe. It includes a cup of Shaoxing wine, a quarter cup of sesame oil and a cup of dark sweet soy sauce (San Bei Ji). Serve this dish with a bowl of hot steamed rice for a fast dinner.

Details

Prep Time: 20-30 minutes

Cooking Time: 10 minutes

Serves: 4

Kcal per serve: 800

Ingredients

- 14.0 oz of boneless, skinless chicken thigh
- ¼ cup of all-purpose flour
- 1 cup of dark sweet soy sauce
- ¼ cup of light soy sauce
- 1 cup of chicken broth
- ¼ cup sesame oil
- 3 garlic cloves, minced
- ½ cup of shallots, 1-inch chunks
- 1 fresh cayenne pepper
- 1 tbsp. of grated ginger
- ¼ cup of chopped scallions
- 3 cups of coconut oil

Preparation

1. Slice the scallions thinly to get a quarter of a cup. Peel and chop the shallots into 1-inch chunks and measure to fill half a cup. Peel the garlic but do not crush them. Peel and grate the ginger root to fill 2 teaspoons. Cut the fresh cayenne pepper to 2-inch pieces. Remove the seeds and stem.

2. Cut the boneless, skinless chicken thigh to bite-sized pieces. Divide the flour into two bowls. Mix the first bowl of flour with a pinch of salt and pepper. Take 2 tablespoons of chicken broth and mix with the flour in the second bowl to make a thick paste. Coat the chicken thigh in the dry mix, then to the wet mixture.

3. Heat a non-stick pan over medium heat; pour coconut oil or other vegetable oil that can stand high heat. Make sure the oil covers at least 1 inch from the bottom of the pan. Once the oil is hot enough, deep fry the chicken thigh for 2-3 minutes or until the coating starts to harden and turns golden brown. Dry them on a kitchen towel to absorb some of the oil.

4. Now prepare the garlic. While the oil is still hot, deep fry the garlic until streaks of brownish yellow appear on the surface. Turn off the heat.

5. Prepare a bowl for the sauce mixture. Mix together the dark soy sauce, light soy sauce, sesame oil, the rest of the chicken stock, Shaoxing wine and grated ginger.

6. Combine the chicken, sauce, garlic, shallots, and cayenne pepper in the Instant Pot.

7. Cover and cook on high pressure for 10 minutes.

8. Let the pressure release naturally.

9. Open the lid and simmer to thicken the sauce.

10. Serve in individual bowls over hot steamed rice, sprinkled with chopped scallions along with some steamed or stir-fried vegetables.

Sweet honey and lime barbecue chicken

A gourmet's favourite barbecued sweet honey and lime chicken, is quick and easy one to make. Using honey, soy sauce, mustard, lime juice, tomato paste, mustard, herbs and brown sugar to make the sauce rich and taste, will make wonders to your guest's taste buds. Its ingredients are inexpensive and simple to find.

Details

Prep Time: 15-25 minutes

Cooking Time: 10 minutes

Serves: 4

Kcal per serve: 860

Ingredients

- 17.5 oz (500 gr) boneless chicken thigh
- ½ tablespoon of melted butter
- 1 cup of soy sauce
- ½ cup of honey
- 1 tablespoon brown sugar
- 1 tablespoon lime juice
- 2 medium-sized onions
- ½ tablespoon minced garlic
- ½ tablespoon French mustard
- 2 tablespoons tomato sauce
- 2 tsp. smoked paprika powder
- ½ teaspoon ground cumin
- 2 cups of chopped baby potatoes
- 1 cup of baby carrots
- ½ cup chicken stock
- salt and pepper to taste

Preparation

1. In a small bowl, mix the soy sauce, honey, lime juice, French mustard, smoked paprika powder, ground cumin, tomato paste and a pinch of salt and pepper. Add the butter. In a microwave, warm the sauce until the butter softens. Stir with a spoon until it melts completely into the sauce.

2. Wash the baby potatoes, onions, and baby carrots well. Remove any bruised part. Cut each baby potato into two or three sections. Halve the baby carrots into two lengthwise. Cut each medium-sized onion into four parts. Cutting the root vegetables into two or three parts helps speed up the cooking process.

3. Place the boneless chicken thighs, baby potatoes, quartered onions, and halved baby carrots inside the Instant Pot.

4. Pour the sauce together with the chicken stock in and stir to coat all ingredients.

5. Cover and cook on high pressure for 10 minutes.

6. Let the pressure release naturally.

7. Serve this sweet honey and lime barbecue chicken with the potatoes, carrots, and onions.

Cooking tips

Choose replacing the chicken thigh for turkey or chicken breast. Optionally, use softer vegetables like eggplant or zucchini. Steam them separately to avoid overcooking then toss altogether into the barbecue sauce before serving.

Chicken Hainanese

Flavorful, fragrant, gelatinous... chicken simply poached to perfection. A Hainan original dish that you can enjoy at home, exactly as you would, right from any local Singaporean hawker stall. This simple-to-prepare dish is a must-try!

Details

Preparation Time: 20 minutes

Cooking Time: 4 hours

Serves: 4

Kcal per serve: 550

Ingredients

- 1 Whole Chicken
- 1 thumb-sized Piece Ginger, peeled and thinly sliced
- 6 cloves Garlic, crushed
- 6 pieces Pandan Leaves/cilantro bundled
- 1 tsp. Salt
- 1 tbsp. Sesame Oil

Ginger Dip
- 2 tbsp. minced Ginger
- 1 tsp. minced Garlic
- 1 tbsp. Chicken Stock
- 1 tsp. Sesame Oil
- ½ tsp. Sugar
- Salt, to taste

Preparation

1. Combine chicken, garlic, ginger, pandan leaves, and salt in the pot.

2. Add enough water to fully submerge the chicken and cook on slow cooker mode set to low for 4 hours.

3. Carefully take chicken out of the pot and chill in an ice bath for 10 minutes.

4. Meanwhile, combine all ingredients for the ginger dip in a food processor and pulse into a coarse paste.

5. Take the chicken out of the ice bath, drain, and chop into serving pieces. Arrange onto a serving platter and brush with sesame oil.

6. Serve chicken with ginger dip on the side.

Cooking tips

For an authentic Malayan dining experience, be sure to shock the cooked chicken in an ice bath for that distinct gelatinous finish. Then serve the main course paired with long-grain rice cooked in the poaching stock, a dip of Kecap Manis (an Indonesian sweetened soy sauce), a chili-based condiment, and a bowl of clear soup topped with crispy fried shallots.

Poached chicken in coconut and lime cream Sauce

Perfectly moist chicken pieces in a creamy coconut and lime poaching sauce. Creamy and tangy, rich yet light, spicy and cool at the same time... Asian cuisines do have their wonders.

Details

Preparation time: 5 minutes

Cooking Time: 10 minutes

Serves: 4

Kcal per serve: 550

Ingredients

- 1 Whole Chicken, cut into serving pieces
- 1 Shallot, minced & cilantro for garnish
- thumb-sized piece Ginger, thinly sliced
- 4 Banana Peppers
- 1 cup Coconut Milk
- ½ cup Chicken Stock
- Juice and Zest of 1 Lime
- 1 tablespoon Fish Sauce

Preparation

1. Combine all ingredients inside the pot.

2. Cook on high pressure for 10 minutes. Release pressure.

3. Top with fresh cilantro.

Cooking tips

Using bone-in pieces of chicken does make for a very notable difference in flavor. And for those who prefer spicier dishes, simply chop up those banana peppers before adding them into the pot.

Tamarind and lemongrass braised chicken

Rendering a deep-flavoured chicken broth can only be done through a long and slow braise, resulting in truly rewarding results. Add in the fruity tang of tamarind, the citrusy notes of lemongrass, and the soothing warmth of turmeric and you've got a dish every bit worthy of being classified as comfort food.

Details

Preparation Time: 5 minutes

Cooking Time: 4 hours

Serves: 4

Kcal per serve: 815

Ingredients

- 6 Chicken Thighs, bone-in
- 1 stalk Lemongrass, bruised and bundled-up
- 2 tablespoons Tamarind Paste
- 1 thumb-sized piece Fresh Turmeric, cut into thin strips
- 4 cups Chicken Stock
- 4 Roma Tomatoes, quartered
- 2 Shallots, quartered
- 4 Banana Peppers
- 1 Radish, peeled and chopped into 2" batons
- a handful Mustard Leaves
- Salt or Fish Sauce to taste

Preparation

1. Combine all ingredients inside the pot.

2. Cook on slow cooker mode set low for 4 hours. Release pressure.

3. Add the mustard leaves and leave to wilt for a few minutes over keep warm setting.

Cooking tips

In the absence of fresh turmeric, ginger may be used along with a pinch of turmeric powder. And just like with any braised chicken dish, choosing an older, tougher bird, would be ideal for deeper flavor.

Chilli Recipes

||||||||||||||||||||||||||||||||||||||||||||||||||||

Bean and chickpea chilli

||||||||||||||||||||||||||||||||||||||||||||||||||||||||||||||||||||||||||||||||||||||||||||||||

A quick and delicious vegetarian chilli that's easy to prepare and is packed with healthy protein from the beans and chickpeas. For extra spiciness add extra jalapeños and some cayenne pepper. Serve it with diced avocado, corn tortilla chips, shredded green onions and grated vegetarian cheese.

Details

Preparation Time: 10 minutes

Cooking Time: 15 minutes

Serves: 2

Kcal per serve: 870

Ingredients

- 1 tbsp. olive oil
- 1 red onion, diced
- 4 cloves garlic, minced
- 1 medium red bell pepper, deseeded and diced
- 2 jalapeño peppers, deseeded and diced
- 2 cups vegetable stock
- 14 oz. frozen whole kernel corn, defrosted
- 1 can (14.5oz.) chopped tomatoes
- 2 cups canned cannellini beans, drained
- 1 ½ cups canned chickpeas, drained
- 2 tsp. chilli powder, or to taste
- 1 tsp. ground cumin
- 1 tsp. smoked paprika
- 1 tsp. dried oregano
- 1 tsp. dried thyme
- ½ tsp. black pepper
- ¼ tsp. salt
- 2 tbsp. cilantro, chopped
- 8 oz. vegetarian cream cheese

Preparation

1. Set the instant pot to Sauté (normal) and add the olive oil. When hot add the onions, garlic, bell peppers and jalapeño peppers and sauté for 2 – 3 minutes until the onions are soft.

2. Add the remaining ingredients, except the cream cheese, to the pot. Set to manual (normal) for 10 minutes. When done do a quick release of the pressure.

3. Set the Instant Pot to Sauté (less/low) and add the cream cheese. Stir in the cream cheese to incorporate into the sauce, about 2 minutes.

Cooking tips

Reduce calories and use fat-free cream cheese. You can substitute the frozen whole kernel corn with canned corn (drained). For the best flavor cut kernels from whole fresh corn cob when available.

Lentil, broccoli and & okra curry

|||||||||||||||||||||||||||||||||||||||||||||||||||||||||||||||||||||||||||||||||||||||||||||||||||||||||||||||||||||

A hearty vegetarian taste of South Asia that's bursting with flavor and wholesome ingredients. You can spice it up by adding a couple of sliced chilies and some red chili pepper flakes. It's a versatile recipe so experiment by adding broad beans, corn kernels or diced cabbage.

Details

Preparation Time: 10 minutes

Cooking Time: 20 minutes

Serves: 2

Kcal per serve: 440

Ingredients

- 2 tbsp. olive oil
- 1 red onion, diced
- 3 cloves garlic, minced
- 1 red bell pepper, sliced
- 1 tsp. cumin seeds
- 1 tsp. fennel seeds
- 1 tsp. ground ginger
- 1 tsp. ground coriander
- 1 tsp. curry powder (mild or hot)
- ¼ tsp. black pepper
- salt to taste
- 2 ½ cups vegetable stock
- 1 tbsp. tomato paste
- 1 can (14 oz.) crushed tomatoes
- ½ cup coconut milk
- 1 cup brown lentils, rinsed
- 1 cup broccoli florets
- 1 cup okra/1+1 cup cornstarch & water
- 2 tbsp. cilantro, chopped

Preparation

1. Set the instant pot to Sauté (normal) and add the olive oil. When hot add the onions and sauté for 2 minutes until soft. Add the garlic, bell peppers, fennel and cumin seeds, ginger, coriander, curry powder, black pepper and salt to taste and sauté for another 2 minutes.

2. Add the vegetable stock, tomato paste, crushed tomatoes, coconut milk and lentils and stir to combine.

3. Add the broccoli and okra and stir in. Set the Instant Pot to Manual (Normal) for 6 minutes. When done allow the pressure to release naturally for 10 minutes. Do a quick release of any remaining pressure and remove the lid.

4. Stir in the cilantro and serve.

Cooking tips

You can use frozen cut okra if fresh okra is not available. Canned okra will also be ok to use but frozen is preferable. Use ¾ of a 14 oz. can of sliced okra, drained before using.

Penne all'arrabiata

Have this easy to prepare spicy vegetarian pasta dish on your table in less than half an hour! Perfect for those busy mid-week days when just don't have the time to spend in the kitchen. A ready-made marinara sauce is used as a time-saver but why not try it with home-made marinara sauce when you have the time.

Details

Preparation Time: 5 minutes

Cooking Time: 15 minutes

Serves: 4

Kcal per serve: 550

Ingredients

- 1 tbsp. olive oil
- 1 small onion, diced
- 3 cloves garlic, minced
- 1 zucchini, halved and ¾" sliced
- ½ cup dry white wine, or water
- 2 red chilies, deseeded and chopped
- 1 tsp. Italian herb seasoning
- ½ tsp. red chili flakes, or to taste
- 1 tbsp. fresh basil, chopped (or 1tsp. dried)
- 1 tbsp. fresh parsley, chopped (or 1 tsp. dried)
- 3 cups vegetarian marinara sauce
- salt and black pepper to taste
- 16 oz. penne

Preparation

1. Select Sauté (less) and add the olive oil. When hot add the onions and sauté for 2 minutes until soft. Add the garlic and zucchini and sauté for a further minute. Add the wine and deglaze the base of the pot. Switch the Instant Pot off.

2. Add the remaining ingredients except the pasta and stir to combine. Season to taste with salt and black pepper.

3. Add the pasta and stir in, ensuring that it is covered by sauce.

4. Set the instant pot to manual (low) for 5 minutes. When done allow the pressure to release naturally for 5 minutes before doing a quick release of the remaining pressure.

Cooking tips

The cooking time at low pressure should be half the cooking time on the package of pasta. If the pasta is still undercooked after pressure cooking set the Instant Pot to Sauté (normal), add some water if necessary and simmer until the pasta is cooked to your preference.

Linguini with mixed mushroom ragout

They're high in antioxidants, they speed up the metabolism, and are low-calorie. It is a fact that mushrooms are wonderfully healthy... and this simple dish only proves that they can also be yummy! Too good to be true?

Details

Preparation Time: 15 minutes

Cooking Time: 4 hours

Serves: 2

Kcal per serve: 715

Ingredients

- 1lb (450gr) Mushrooms cleaned and sliced
- 1 White Onion, chopped
- 6 cloves Garlic, minced
- 1 teaspoon Ground Black Pepper
- 1.5 cups Vegetable Stock
- ½ cup Red Wine
- 1 can Diced Tomatoes
- 2 tablespoons Chopped Basil
- 2 tablespoons Olive Oil
- 9 oz (250 gr) Linguini, cooked to package directions
- Salt, to taste

Preparation

1. Set pot to slow cooker mode on low.

2. Combine mushrooms, onions, pepper, vegetable stock, red wine, tomatoes, basil, and diced tomatoes inside the pot.

3. Cook for 4 hours.

4. Season with salt to taste.

5. Ladle over hot linguini.

6. Top with a drizzle of olive oil before serving.

Cooking tips

Make this ragout even healthier by using your favorite gluten-free pasta. Top with some shaved parmesan or chopped fresh herbs to elevate the flavors even further. For some heat, a pinch of red pepper flakes would be great!

Coconut and chili green beans

A quick and easy Asian vegetable stir-fry conveniently adapted for the Instant Pot. Creamy and perfectly spicy, this all-in-one dish will surely awaken the taste buds!

Details

Preparation Time: 10 minutes

Cooking Time: 15 minutes

Serves: 2

Kcal per serve: 850

Ingredients

- 1lb (450gr) Green Beans, cut into ½" pieces
- 1/2 lb.(225gr) Ground Pork
- 1.5 cups Coconut Milk
- 4 cloves Garlic, minced
- 1 Shallot, thinly sliced
- 2-3 Pieces Red Thai Chili, chopped
- 1 tablespoon Fish

Preparation

1. Set pot to sauté mode.

2. Heat coconut oil.

3. Add ground pork and sauté until slightly brown.

4. Put the shallots, the garlic and of course the chili. Sauté well until aromatic.

5. Add green beans and sauté until a bit tender.

6. Add coconut milk and fish sauce. Simmer for 5 minutes.

Cooking tips

To suit a strict vegetarian diet, pan-fried tofu may be substituted for the ground pork. Vegan varieties of fish sauce can also be easily had from most specialty health shops.

Instant pot beef chili stuffed peppers

This beef chili stuffed peppers recipe is easy and versatile. A variety of ground meat may be used for the stuffing, filling the peppers up and cook into the Instant Pot. Turkey and chicken are also great options. Adjust the liquid and cooking time accordingly, as ground turkey and chicken tend to cook faster and are mushier compared to ground beef.

Details

Prep time: 30-45 min.

Cooking time: 10 min.

Serves: 2

Kcal per serve: 580

Ingredients

- 6 medium-sized sweet bell peppers
- 100 grams of ground beef (3.5 oz)
- ¼ cup of chopped onions
- ¼ cup of sliced jalapeños
- ¼ cup of crushed tomatoes
- 2 tablespoons of tomato sauce
- 1 teaspoon of chili powder
- 1 teaspoon of ground black pepper
- 1 teaspoon of cumin
- 1 tablespoon of Worcestershire sauce
- ½ tablespoon of cornstarch
- 1 tablespoon of olive oil
- 1 tablespoon of beef broth
- 1-2 cups of beef broth to cover peppers
- ½ cup of shredded cheddar
- salt and pepper to taste

Preparation

1. Wash and dry your sweet bell peppers. Cut the top, remove the stem and seeds.
2. Peel and chop the onions. Slice the jalapeños. Open the canned tomatoes. Measure the rest of the ingredients according to instructions.
3. Dilute cornstarch in 1 tablespoon of beef broth, set aside.

4. Set the Instant Pot to sauté.

5. Add the olive oil and sauté the ground beef until evenly browned.

6. Add the onions and sauté until translucent.

7. Add the cumin, ground black pepper, chili powder, crushed tomatoes, tomato sauce, and Worcestershire sauce. Season with some salt.

8. Add the cornstarch slurry and simmer until thick.

9. Transfer the stuffing out of the pot into a plate. Leave to cool for 10-15 minutes.

10. Stuff the sweet bell peppers with the beef mixture, push slightly so that each pepper will have a dense ground beef mixture inside.

11. Arrange the stuffed bell peppers back into the pot.
12. Carefully pour a cup of beef broth in, adding more as needed (liquid should at least cover the peppers an inch from the bottom).
13. Cover and cook for 10 minutes on manual.
14. Leave to release pressure naturally.
15. Sprinkle each pepper with shredded cheddar cheese and continue cooking on manual until cheese is melted.

Cooking tips

If you prefer a leaner dish you can trim off any excess fat from the lamb shanks. I particularly like the fatty richness, so I don't. Don't risk substituting Sherry vinegar with red wine vinegar; it will just not taste as good. Sherry vinegar is something you should have in the food cupboard and will once you taste it!

Potato and tofu stuffed chilies

|||||||||||||||||||||||||||||||||||||||||||||||||||||||||||||||||||||||||||||||||||||||||||||||||||||||||||||||||||||||||||||||||||||||||||||

This recipe brings some spice to your meal. These peppers are stuffed with habaneros, cashews, brown sugar and lemon juice. Serve with your favorite bread and taste the creative flavors melding together.

Details

Preparation + Cooking: 30 minutes

Serves: 4

Kcal per serve: 575

Ingredients

- 3 large red bell peppers
- 3 large yellow bell peppers
- 3 large capsicums
- 2 medium-sized onions, finely chopped
- 1 habanero pepper, finely chopped
- 6 large potatoes, boiled and mashed
- 3.5 oz (100 gr) tofu, mashed
- 1 cup green peas, boiled
- 1 tablespoon brown sugar
- 5-6 cashews, grinded
- Salt and black pepper, as per taste
- Handful of coriander leaves
- Juice of half lemon

Preparation

1. Wash and pat dry the bell peppers. Make a cut on top and remove the upper edge, thereby making them hollow. Keep them aside.

2. Set the instant pot to sauté.

3. Pour olive oil in and sauté the onions and habanero peppers until onions turn translucent.

4. Add in the tofu and mashed potatoes. Mix well.

5. Season with salt and pepper. Cook for 3-4 minutes then add the peas, brown sugar, cashews, and cumin powder. Cook for 5 minutes then transfer to a bowl and set aside to cool.

6. Add the chopped coriander leaves and lemon juice into the mixture. Mix well.

7. Fill the peppers with the potato mixture.

8. Arrange the stuffed peppers upright into the instant Pot.

9. Carefully pour in water until about an inch high from the bottom of the pot.

10. Pour some soy sauce and vinegar in.

11. Cover and cook on manual for 10 minutes.

Cooking tips

Consider combining chicken or beef mince in the filling before stuffing the peppers. Choose not stuffing the peppers, but instead chopping them finely and cooking them with the filling. Mix some tomato ketchup with sour cream and add to the peppers on top or mix it with the filling. This will add a tangy twist to the hot habanero.

Butternut, black bean & sweet potato chili

||||||||||||||||||||||||||||||||||||||||||||||||||||||||||||||||||||||||||||||||||||||||||||||||||||

This hearty and warming chili will satisfy both vegetarian and meat lovers. It's a healthy, low calorie and low fat vegetarian alternative that you can make as hot or as mild as you prefer. Experiment with different beans such as cannellini, butter, pinto or red kidney beans. Chickpeas will add extra texture and a nutty flavour.

Details

Prep Time: 20 minutes

Cooking Time: 10 minutes

Serves: 2

Kcal per serve: 450

Ingredients

- 1 large onion
- 2 bell peppers, diced
- 5 garlic cloves, crushed
- 2 tbsp. olive oil
- 2 cups butternut, medium dice
- 2 cans black beans, drained (15oz.)
- 3 cups vegetable stock
- 1 sweet potato, peeled and diced
- 3 ½ cups chopped tomatoes
- 1 tsp. picante (hot) smoked paprika
- 2 tsp. ground chipotle chili pepper
- 1 tsp. ground cumin
- 2 bay leaves
- 1 tsp. chili or cayenne powder
- 1 ½ tbsp. cilantro
- 1 tbsp. parsley, chopped
- 1 ½ tsp. oregano
- Salt and pepper

Garnish
- 1 tbsp. parsley
- ½ tbsp. cilantro, chopped
- 1 cup sour cream or créme fraiche
- 1 tbsp. chopped chives
- 4 sliced onions

Preparation

1. Set the instant pot to sauté.

2. Heat olive oil.

3. Sauté onions, peppers, and garlic until onions are translucent.

4. Add the remaining ingredients and stir to combine.

5. Cover and cook on manual for 10 minutes.

6. Meanwhile, combine the sour cream/créme fraiche, cilantro, chives, and green onions in a bowl. Season with salt and pepper to taste.

7. To serve, sprinkle with chopped parsley and a dollop of the sour créme fraiche mixture on each serving.

Cooking tips

If butternut is unavailable, replace it with peeled pumpkin. Reduce fat and calories by using plain, Greek-style yogurt for the garnish instead of the sour créme fraiche. Add extra sweetness with a cup of frozen corn or peas.

Paprika chicken chili

An easy and versatile Spanish-influenced dish that will give your taste buds a spicy, zingy treat. Make it as hot or as mild to suit your taste: add or substitute with your favorite fresh or dried chili. Serve with plain rice or creamy mashed potato and a simple green salad. Add ½ a cup each of chickpeas and chopped almonds to give the dish extra texture and nuttiness.

Details

Prep Time: 20 minutes
Cooking Time: 10 minutes
Serves: 6
Kcal per serve: 960

Ingredients

- 2.2lb. chicken drumsticks or thighs
- olive oil for frying,
- 3 stalks celery, diced
- 1 green and 1 red bell pepper, diced
- 1 large red onion, diced
- 5 garlic cloves,
- 2 cups chicken stock
- 2 fresh red chilies, thinly sliced
- 1 large carrot, peeled and diced
- ¼ cup sweet Sherry
- 1x(14.5oz. can) chopped tomatoes
- 1 ¾ cups tomato passata,
- 1 can red kidney beans
- 2 tsp. chili powder / ground chipotle chilies
- 2 dried Peppers, halve
- 1 tbsp. picante (hot) smoked paprika
- 6 – 8 sprigs fresh thyme,
- ½ cup toasted almonds
- 1 small bunch flat-leaf parsley, chopped
- Salt and black pepper

Preparation

1. Set Instant Pot to sauté and heat 2 tablespoons of olive oil.

2. Working in batches, sear the chicken pieces until brown on both sides. Set aside.

3. Add 2 more tablespoons of olive oil and sauté the celery, peppers, onion, garlic, and carrot until softened, about 5 minutes.

4. Add the chicken back into the pot together with the rest of the ingredients.

5. Cover and cook for 10 minutes on high pressure.

6. Let the pressure release naturally.

7. Transfer to a serving dish and garnish with parsley.

8. Optional: If desired, you can thicken the sauce with a light corn flour or arrowroot starch slurry.

Fish Recipes

||||||||||||||||||||||||||||||||||||||||||||||

Clam chowder

A thick and creamy clam chowder with a real wow factor! This delicious chowder is a perfect winter soup but can also be enjoyed all year round. Smoky bacon and fresh thyme flavors perfectly complement the clams. Serve with a loaf of fresh crusty bread or soup crackers.

Details

Preparation Time: 10 minutes

Cooking Time: 20 minutes

Serves: 4

Kcal per serve: 610

Ingredients

- 1 tbsp. butter
- ½ cup smoked dry-cured bacon or pancetta, diced
- 1 medium white onion
- 1 stalk celery, diced
- 2 cloves garlic, minced
- ½ cup dry white wine
- 2 cups (16 fl. oz.) clam juice
- 2 medium potatoes, peeled and diced
- 2 bay leaves
- 2 sprigs fresh thyme
- ⅓ tsp. freshly ground black pepper
- 2 cups half and half
- 11 oz. canned whole baby clams, dried liquid reserved
- sea salt to taste
- 1 -2 tbsp. cornstarch dissolved in water

Preparation

1. Set the instant pot to Sauté (less/low) and add the butter and bacon (or pancetta). Sauté for 3 minutes. Add the onion and celery and sauté for another 2 minutes. Add the garlic and sauté for another minute. Add the wine and cook for a further minute, or until reduced by half, stirring to scrap off any bits stuck to the bottom of the pot.

2. Add the liquid from the canned clams, clam juice, potatoes, bay leaves, thyme and pepper. Set the instant pot to manual (more/high) for 5 minutes. When done release the pressure manually and remove the lid.

3. Set the instant pot to Sauté (less) and stir in the half and half and clams. Simmer for 5 minutes, stirring occasionally. Taste and add salt if desired. Remove the thyme stalks and bay leaves.

4. Gradually add the cornstarch mixture, stirring constantly, until you have the desired thickness.

Cooking tips

You can make your own half and half by blending together equal quantities of whole milk and single cream. For richer tasting chowder use 1 ½ cups single cream and ½ cup whole milk.

Fusilli pasta with tuna & olives

||||||||||||||||||||||||||||||||||||||||||||||||||||||||||||||||||||||||||||||||||||||||||||||||||

Prepare this family favorite taste of Italy from pantry-store ingredients in less time than it normally takes to boil the pasta. When you've had a busy day and the thought of spending ages in the kitchen to feed the family this is the perfect recipe. A grated bowl of Parmesan is all you need to add.

Details

Preparation Time: 10 minutes
Cooking Time: 7 minutes
Serves: 2
Kcal per serve: 780

Ingredients

- 1 tbsp. olive oil
- 3 anchovy fillets
- 1 medium red onion, diced
- 3 cloves garlic, minced
- 2 cups tomato passata
- 12 Kalamata olives, halved
- 2 tbsp. capers
- 1 tsp. dried basil
- 1 tsp. dried oregano
- ⅓ cup parsley chopped (reserve a tbsp. for finishing)
- ⅓ tsp. black pepper or to taste
- ½ tsp. red chili flakes, or to taste
- 2 cans (5 oz.) tuna in olive oil
- 16 oz. fusilli pasta

Preparation

1. Set the instant pot to Sauté (normal) and add the olive oil and anchovy fillets. Stir the anchovy fillets until they have disintegrated. Add the onions and sauté for 2 minutes or until softened. Add the garlic and sauté for another minute.

2. Add the tomato passata, olives, capers, basil, oregano, parsley, pepper and chili flakes. Stir in one can of tuna until broken down and incorporated into the tomato passata.

3. Add the fusilli and stir in. Smooth the pasta to an even layer. Add just enough water to cover the pasta.

4. Secure the lid with the steam vent off and set the Instant Pot to manual (less/low) for 5 minutes (see Cook's tip). Do a quick release of the pressure?

5. Add the remaining parsley and can of tuna and stir in. No salt was added in the cooking process as the anchovies, tuna, capers and olives are all salty so taste and add to taste if desired.

6. Serve with a bowl of grated parmesan cheese and a drizzle of extra virgin olive oil.

Cooking tips

The cooking time at low pressure should be half the cooking time on the package of pasta. If the pasta is still undercooked after pressure cooking set the Instant Pot to Sauté (normal), add some water and simmer until the pasta is cooked to your preference. Do this before step 5.

Mussels Normandy

This classic dish of the northern apple-growing region of France, Normandy, has become a favorite all over the world. The freshest of mussels, with their salty taste of the sea, is the key to creating a memorable dish. Add a dash or two of Calvados with the crème fraiche at the end for extra authenticity.

Details

Preparation Time: 20 minutes

Cooking Time: 11 minutes

Serves: 4

Kcal per serve: 700

Ingredients

- 1 tbsp. butter
- 3 oz. dry cured smoked bacon, diced
- 1 medium white onion, finely diced
- 2 cloves garlic, minced
- 2 cups hard dry cider
- 1 tsp. fresh thyme, chopped
- salt and black pepper to taste
- 4 lb. mussels, scrubbed and de-bearded
- ¼ cup parsley, chopped
- ½ cup crème fraiche

Preparation

1. Set the instant pot to Sauté (normal) and add the butter. When hot add the bacon and sauté for 2 minutes. Add the onion and garlic and sauté for another 2 minutes.

2. Add the cider, thyme, salt and pepper and simmer for about 5 minutes, or until the liquid has reduced by half. Add the mussels.

3. Secure the lid with the steam vent closed and set the pot to manual (more/high) for 1 minute. When done do a quick release of the pressure and remove the lid.

4. Remove the mussels with a slotted spoon to a warm serving dish. Discard any unopened mussels.

5. Set the pot to Sauté (more/high). Add and stir in the parsley and crème fraiche. Taste and season with salt and pepper if desired. Bring the sauce to the boil. Switch the pot off.

6. Pour the sauce over the mussels.

Cooking tips

If you need to store the fresh mussels for a day or two first remove them from any plastic packaging. Place them in a bowl and cover with damp kitchen paper or a damp dish cloth. Place in the bottom of the fridge. Discard any that stay open when firmly tapped.

Shrimp paella

||||||||||||||||||||||||||||||||||||||||||||||||||||||||||||||||||||||||||||||||||||||||||||||||||||||||||||||||

Try this delicious paella recipe when you don't feel like spending an hour preparing paella the traditional way. It has loads of flavor and it will be on the table in less than half an hour. The next time you cook this dish try experimenting and add other seafood such as clams and scallops.

Details

Preparation Time: 10 minutes

Cooking Time: 13 minutes

Serves: 2

Kcal per serve: 650

Ingredients

- 1 tbsp. extra virgin olive oil
- 1 tbsp. butter
- 1 lb. jumbo shrimp, shell on
- 1 medium onion, diced
- 4 cloves garlic, minced
- 1 medium red bell pepper, deseeded and diced
- 1 cup Paella rice
- ½ cup dry white wine
- 1 cup fish stock
- ⅓ cup marinara sauc
- 1 large pinch saffron threads
- 1 tsp. smoked paprika
- ½ cup parsley, chopped
- salt and black pepper to taste
- parsley for garnish
- lemon wedges for garnish

Preparation

1. Set the instant pot to Sauté (normal) and add the olive oil and butter. When hot add the onions and sauté for 2 minutes until softened. Add the garlic and bell pepper and sauté for a further 2 minutes. Add the rice and sauté for another 2 minutes.

2. Add the white wine and simmer for a few minutes, or until reduced by half. Add the fish stock, marinara sauce, saffron, paprika, parsley and salt and pepper to taste.

3. Set the pot to manual (more/high) for 5 minutes. When done do a quick release of the pressure.

4. Serve garnished with a sprinkling of parsley and lemon wedges.

Cooking tips

The best rice for paella is the Spanish "Bomba" rice because it absorbs the liquid but remains relatively firm. If it's not available, you can use short-grained white rice. Don't use risotto Arborio rice as it goes too 'creamy'.

Steamed cod Mediterranean style

This delicious and healthy taste of the Mediterranean that's fragrant with fresh rosemary and thyme is on the table in less than half an hour. The salty tartness of the olives and capers add excitement to the sweet cherry tomatoes. This recipe is also great for other white fish such as tilapia or pollack and even salmon.

Details

Preparation Time: 10 minutes

Cooking Time: 5 minutes

Serves: 2

Kcal per serve: 700

Ingredients

- 4 cod fillets (about 2 lb.)
- 2 tbsp. extra virgin olive oil
- 2 cloves garlic, minced
- 1 lb. ripe cherry tomatoes, halved
- 1 cup pitted Kalamata olives
- 2 tbsp. capers
- 4 green onions, sliced
- 6 sprigs thyme
- 4 sprigs rosemary
- Salt and black pepper

Preparation

1. Add the tomatoes and green onions to a bowl and season with salt and pepper. Add 1 tbsp. oliv oil and coat the tomatoes and green onions. Spread a layer of ½ the tomato and green onion mixture in the steamer basket and top with ½ the thyme and rosemary.

2. Brush the cod fillets with the remaining olive oil and season with salt and pepper on both sides. Note that the olives and capers are salty. Place onto the layer of the tomato mixture in the steamer basket.

3. Sprinkle over the remaining tomato-green onion mixture, the olives, capers and herbs.

4. Pour a cup of water into the Instant Pot, add the steamer basket and set to Manual (less/low) for 5 minutes. When done do a quick release of the pressure.

5. Remove the fish to a serving dish. Remove the rosemary and thyme sprigs and pour the tomato, olive, caper and green onion mixture over the fish. Drizzle with extra virgin olive oil and garnish with rosemary and thyme sprigs.

Cooking tips

Add another flavor dimension to the dish by adding very thinly sliced fennel bulb, a few lemon slices and two or three sprigs of fresh tarragon or dill on top of the fish fillets. Always use skinless fish fillets.

Mixed seafood moqueca

If you think Brazilian food is all about its mouth-watering barbeque, this native specialty should be enough to make you think again. An assortment of fresh seafood, stewed in rich coconut milk and a fresh blend of herbs and spices... doesn't that just sound as delicious as all their popular meat dishes?

Details

Preparation Time: 10 minutes

Cooking Time: 15 minutes

Serves: 4

Kcal per serve: 700

Ingredients

- 1lb (450gr) Halibut, cut into 2" pieces
- 1lb (450gr) Clams
- 1/2lbs (225 g) Prawns
- 2 cups Coconut Milk
- 4 cloves Garlic, crushed
- Juice of 1 Lime
- 1 tbsp. Olive Oil
- 1 Red Bell Pepper
- 1 Onion, chopped
- 1 cup chopped Tomatoes
- 1 tablespoon Paprika
- 1 teaspoon Red Chili Flakes
- 1 bunch Cilantro, roughly chopped Salt, to taste

Preparation

1. Set pot to sauté mode.

2. Heat olive oil.

3. Sauté onions, bell pepper, red chili flakes, and garlic until onions turn translucent.

4. Add the clams. Cover and leave to steam until the clam shells open.

5. Add the coconut milk and chopped tomatoes. Bring to a simmer.

6. Add the fish and prawns. Simmer for 5-7 minutes.

7. Season with salt.

8. Press and juice in fresh lime juice, topped with chopped fresh cilantro before serving it.

Cooking tips

The key to a good Moqueca, or any seafood dish in general, is simple – to use only the freshest ingredients. It would always be better to substitute local catch into this recipe, going for cod or swordfish in lace of halibut, for example.

Salmon poached in ginger-miso broth

The earthiness of mushrooms, umami-rich tandem of miso and dashi, and soothingly warm ginger form the perfect poaching base for a truly exquisite salmon dish. Elegance in pure simplicity... this Japanese-inspired dish perfectly mirrors their minimalist culture.

Details

Preparation Time: 10 Minutes

Cooking Time: 10 minutes

Serves: 1

Kcal per serve: 720

Ingredients

- 2 Salmon Fillet Steaks
- 1 cup Dried Shiitake Mushrooms, pre-soaked
- 1 thumb-sized piece Ginger thinly sliced
- ¼ cup Scallions, chopped
- 2 tablespoons Miso Paste
- 2 cups Dashi Stock
- a handful Enoki Mushrooms
- 1 teaspoon Sesame Oil

Preparation

1. Set pot to sauté mode.

2. Heat vegetable oil and sauté ginger for a minute.

3. Add dashi stock, miso, and shiitake mushrooms. Bring to a simmer.

4. Switch pot to keep warm setting.

5. Add the salmon fillets and enoki mushrooms. Leave to poach at 165F for 8-10 minutes. Adjust poaching time depending on desired doneness of the salmon.

6. Drizzle in the sesame oil before serving.

Cooking tips

Cooking time for the salmon would depend on the size of the fillets used and of course your desired doneness. Going for an internal temperature reading of 145F with a meat thermometer inserted into the thickest part of the fish, would be ideal for precise results.

Black bean and chili steamed tilapia

White fillets of Tilapia, topped with a blanket of Oriental flavors, set on a bed of aromatics, and left to steam until perfectly delicate. A restaurant-quality fish dinner out of your very own Instant Pot.

Details

Preparation Time: 10 minutes
Cooking Time: 2 minutes
Serves: 1
Kcal per Serve: 600

Ingredients

- 2 Tilapia Fillets
- 2 tablespoons Fermented Black Beans, chopped
- 1-2 Thai chilis, chopped
- 1 tablespoon minced Ginger
- 1 Shallot, thinly sliced
- 2 tablespoons Oyster Sauce
- 1 teaspoon Sesame Oil
- 1 teaspoon Brown Sugar
- Leeks

Preparation

1. Toss the black beans, chili, ginger, shallots, oyster sauce, sesame oil, and brown sugar in a bowl.

2. Arrange the leeks at the bottom of the pot, forming a bed for the tilapia fillets.

3. Pour in half a cup of water.

4. Lay the fish on top of the leeks and spoon the black bean mixture on top.

5. Cook on low pressure for 2 minutes. Release pressure.

Cooking tips

Not that much of a preference for tilapia? Most types of grouper and marlin would be excellent as well, if not better choices. Also, be sure to have some extra chopped cilantro for topping off the dish right before serving.

Tomato fish curry

The best strategy for your Instant Pot fish recipes is keeping it simple. This hearty fish curry's secret is cooking the spices slowly with pureed tomatoes and onions, then adding your fish fillets during the final hour. Consider adding potato mash with the onions before putting them in with the fish.

Details

Prep Time: 10 minutes

Cooking Time: 3 minutes

Serves: 2

Kcal per serve: 650

Ingredients

- 1 tablespoon olive or vegetable oil
- 3 medium onions, grinded into paste
- 2 tomatoes, pureed
- An inch of ginger, grated
- 5 garlic cloves, minced
- 1/4 teaspoon crushed red pepper flakes
- 2 teaspoons red chili powder
- ½ teaspoon turmeric powder
- Salt and black pepper, as per taste
- 1 cup tomato sauce
- 2.2 pounds cod filets, into 1-inch pieces

Preparation

1. Set the Instant Pot to sauté.

2. Heat some oil in the pot and add onion paste, tomato puree, ginger and garlic. Add the pepper flakes, salt, and black pepper along with the powdered spices. Sauté for a few minutes then add the tomato sauce and lemon juice.

3. Arrange the cod pieces on top, lock the lid and cook on manual for 3 minutes.

4. Release pressure manually.

5. Serve hot with steamed rice.

Cooking tips

Consider soaking couscous seeds in a pot with water for 30 minutes and then crushing them with a rolling pin. Then put the paste into the pot while the onion paste is cooking. Consider adding two or so boiled, then mashed, potatoes, along with the tomatoes and onions.

Sour cream and Greek yogurt salmon dip

A perfect cooking idea for to use up that leftover salmon fillet, canned salmon or smoked salmon that has been sitting for a couple of days. Thanks to using yogurt and sour cream rather than lemon juice and cream cheese, the calorie count is noticeably reduced. This recipe is rather adaptable, so feel free to add or leave out ingredients to suit your taste. Instead of chives, consider basil, mint or celery.

Details

Prep Time: 20 minutes

Cooking Time: 3 minutes

Serves: 1

Kcal per serve: 550

Ingredients

- 200 grams of salmon fillet or smoked (7.0 oz)
- 200 grams of reduced fat sour cream (7.0 oz)
- ½ cup of plain Greek yogurt
- ½ cup of chopped cucumber
- ½ cup of chopped chives
- 1 tbsp. of onion flakes
- A pinch of salt and pepper to taste

Preparation

1. Peel the cucumber. Remove the seeds as they have the tendency to be watery. Chop your chives to fill half a cup. You may use other types of aromatics such as scallions, basil, celery, or parsley.

2. Cut the smoked salmon or salmon fillet into small bits. Salmon fillets can be quite expensive at times. You can use canned salmon in water or in oil for this recipe. Be sure you drain the fish from the canning liquid well.

3. In the Instant Pot, combine the chopped salmon, sour cream and onion flakes. Add salt and pepper to taste. Cover and cook on manual for 3 minutes. Quick-release pressure.

4. Open the lid then stir in the yogurt. At this point, you can use an immersion blender or transfer the mixture to a regular blender to make the dip creamier. Pulse 2-3 times for a coarser smoked salmon texture and pulse 6-8 times for a smoother dip. Afterwards, add the chopped chives and cucumber.

5. Serve the salmon dip with saltine crackers, baked tortilla chips, veggie sticks, or cheese sticks. If you plan to make batches and keep it in the freezer, omit the cucumber and use the dried herbs instead of fresh ones. This salmon dip keeps well in the freezer for up to 3 months in airtight containers.

Cooking tips

Make this recipe low-fat by using fat-free sour cream, containing 74 calories per 100 grams versus 181 for regular sour cream. Increase the protein content by adding cooked, mashed beans or cooked quinoa. Try other kinds of firm fish fillets as well as white meat.

Steamed banana and coconut tuna with fruit punch

A salmon recipe that will delight your friends and family: cooked in fruits that have been mixed with ground vegetables and wine, a wonderful mix. Pomegranate and orange provide the citrus with flavors while red wine and olives add an exotic aroma. The fish are wrapped inside banana leaves before being steamed in coconut oil and water to produce the mildness and enticing aroma.

Details

Prep Time: 20 minutes

Cooking Time: 3 minutes

Serves: 6

Kcal per serve: 585

Ingredients

- 6 thick full salmon fillets, skin-on
- 2 tablespoons olive oil
- 1/4 cup rose wine
- Salt and black pepper
- 1 orange, mashed
- 2 onions, diced
- 1 large capsicum, diced
- 2 tomatoes, diced
- 5-6 mushrooms, sliced
- 2 teaspoons paprika
- 1 cup pomegranate kernels
- ½ cup black olives
- ½ cup red wine
- 1 cup coconut milk
- 6 equal-sized banana leaves

Preparation

1. Take a mixing bowl and combine the olive oil with wine, salt, pepper and orange pulp (mashed orange).

2. Set the Instant Pot to sauté and pour some olive oil in. Sear the salmon for a couple of minutes on each side. Remove from the pot and keep aside.

3. Pour some more oil into the pot and add the onions in. Sweat until translucent.

4. Add the capsicum, tomatoes, and mushrooms. sauté for a few more minutes.

5. Mix in the paprika, olives and some red wine. Thereafter, add the pomegrenate kernels and mix well. Continue to cook for 5-7 minutes. Turn of the heat.

6. Take the mixture out of the pot and allow to cool to room temperature. Once cool, process in a grinder/blender into a coarse texture.

7. Pour the mixture all over the fish fillets and wrap them in banana leaves.

8. Pour the coconut milk into the Instant Pot and arrange the wrapped fish fillets in.

9. Lock the lid and cook on manual for 3 minutes.

10. Quick-release the pressure out of the pot.

11. Serve hot.

Cooking tips

For more flavour and aroma, when steaming the fish, add lime wedges and lavender sprigs. Before steaming, make a fine paste by grinding yogurt with mint, coriander and salt and then cook the fish fillets in that. It will bring this recipe to a different level.

Tilapia and shrimp multigrain paella

||||||||||||||||||||||||||||||||||||||||||||||||||||||||||||||||||||||||||||||||||||||||||||||||||||||||||||||||

This recipe is a healthier take on the traditional seafood paella that uses white rice. Instead of using white rice, I am using mixed multigrain (lentils, sesame, quinoa, brown rice and Chinese barley). You could use store-bought packaged mix grains or adjust the grains according to your personal preference. You can add and omit ingredients to suit your family's taste and likings.

Details

Prep Time: 15-20 minutes

Cooking Time: 35 minutes

Serves: 4

Kcal per serve: 450

Ingredients

- 1/2 cup of uncooked brown rice
- 1/4 cup of uncooked quinoa
- 1/4 cup of uncooked Job's tears
- 2 tbsps. Uncooked lentils
- 2 tbsps. Sesame seeds
- 2.5 cups of chicken broth
- 7 oz (200 gr) tilapia fillet
- 1/2 cup of shrimps, shelled, deveined
- 1/2 cup of chopped onions
- 1 tbsp. garlic, minced
- 1 tsp. thyme
- 1 tsp. chili flakes
- 1/2 tsp. turmeric powder
- 1 cup of green peas
- 1 cup of sweet Bell peppers, chopped
- 2 tbsp. olive oil
- Salt and pepper to taste

Preparation

1. Wash and chop your sweet bell peppers. Remove the stems and seeds. Pell and chop the onions. Peel and mince the garlic. Cut the tilapia fillets into slightly larger than bite-sized pieces. Wash, peel and devein your shrimp.

2. Season tilapia fillets and shrimps with salt and pepper.

3. Set the instant pot to sauté.

4. Add olive oil and sear tilapia fillets and shrimps until fully cooked. Set aside.

5. Rinse the brown rice and multi grains under cold tap water to wash away debris and inedible hulls that may be present. Drain.

6. In the same pot, add quinoa, lentils, brown rice, sesame seeds, Chinese barley pearls, sweet bell peppers, onions, garlic, turmeric powder, thyme, chili flakes, and chicken broth. Stir well.

7. Lock the lid and cook on manual for 25 minutes.

8. Leave for another 10 minutes before releasing pressure.

9. Top with tilapia fillets, shrimp, and green peas before serving.

Cooking tips

A combination of seeds and grains may be used in this recipe. However, bear in mind that grains absorb more water than seeds, so if you are using a higher ratio of grains to seeds, increase the amount of chicken broth.

Cod and mussel stew

This delicious and versatile Spanish-inspired seafood stew will have your guests queuing up for seconds! You may replace cod for any firm-fleshed white fish, salmon or even a mixture of any fresh firm-fleshed fish that is available. Try not to use delicate fleshed fish as they tend to break up in the stew. Add prawns or clams for some extra seafood luxury.

Details

Prep Time: 25 minutes

Cooking Time: 15 minutes

Serves: 4

Kcal per serve: 530

Ingredients

- 1 tablespoon virgin olive oil
- 1 onion, 1 stalk celery, diced
- 4 cloves garlic, crushed
- 1 red or yellow bell pepper, diced
- 1 mild red chili, de-seeded and chopped
- 7oz. mild Spanish Chorizo, sliced
- 1 can (14oz.) chopped tomatoes
- ½ cup tomato passata
- ¼ cup dry white wine
- ¼ cup fish stock
- 1 tbsp. sweet smoked paprika
- 1 tsp. saffron threads in hot water
- Salt and black pepper, to taste
- 1 tbsp. fresh tarragon, roughly chopped
- 2 tbsp. fresh flat-leaf parsley, chopped
- 1.5lb. fresh mussels, cleaned, de-bearded
- 18 oz. skin-off cod fillets, into 2 ½" cubes
- chopped parsley and tarragon for garnish

Preparation

1. Set the Instant Pot to sauté. Heat olive oil.

2. Add the onion, celery, garlic, bell peppers and chili and gently sauté for a few minutes. Add the chorizo and sauté for another 2-3 minutes. Drain any excess fat if desired.

3. Add the chopped tomatoes, passata, wine, stock, paprika, saffron, salt, and pepper. Cook for 5 minutes, stirring constantly.

4. Add the mussels and fish.

5. Lock the lid and cook on manual for 3 minutes.

6. Quick release pressure manually.

7. Discard any un-opened mussels and garnish with a sprinkling of tarragon and parsley.

Exotic cod curry

||||||||||||||||||||||||||||||||||||||||||||||||||||||||||||||||||||||||||||||||||||||||||||||||||||||||||||||||||||||||||||||||||||||||

An exciting and exotic blend of flavors that will leave your palate wanting more. A perfectly cooked fish in creamy orange hued sauce that is spicy and complex and with depth. With some vegetal notes, the pungent garlic comes through nicely along with the ginger and although bold, the curry doesn't overwhelm.

Details

Prep Time: 25 minutes

Cooking Time: 3 minutes

Serves: 4

Kcal per serve: 720

Ingredients

- 1 ½ lbs. cod fillets, large chunks
- 10 fresh curry leaves
- 6 garlic cloves, minced
- 2 carrots, cut into ¼ inch chunks
- 2 red chilies, finely chopped
- 1 large onion, diced
- 1 red bell pepper, chopped
- 1 bay leaf
- 2 x 15 oz. cans diced tomatoes
- 1 can coconut cream
- Juice of 2 limes
- 3 tablespoons ghee or butter
- 1 tablespoon minced ginger
- 3 teaspoons turmeric powder
- Kosher salt
- Black pepper
- Chopped fresh cilantro, for garnish
- 2 cups cooked rice, for serving

Preparation

1. Set the instant pot to sauté. Heat the ghee.

2. Sauté garlic, chilies, onion, and ginger.

3. Cook while stirring for about a minute. This helps build those pungent base flavors by releasing their natural oils.

4. Add the fish and lightly sear to develop a bit of color on the exterior.

5. Follow with the remaining ingredients except for the cilantro and rice. Season with a generous pinch of salt and black pepper.

6. Lock the lid and cook on manual for 3 minutes.

7. Release pressure naturally.

8. Adjust seasoning as needed.

9. Serve over rice, garnished with fresh cilantro.

Cooking tips

In addition to cod, tilapia works well in this recipe as it does salmon. They both get delightfully and their flavour melds nicely with all the other ingredients in the curry.

Tuna confit caprese salad

||||||||||||||||||||||||||||||||||||||||||||||||||||||||||||||||||||||||||||||||||||||||||||||||||||||||||||||||||||||||

The classic Italian Caprese, made fuller with Tuna fillets that have been poached in extra virgin olive oil and pink peppercorns until perfectly flaky. The flavored confit oil is then whisked with a splash of balsamic vinegar for the perfect vinaigrette.

Details

Preparation Time: 15 minutes

Cooking Time: 4 h

Serves: 2

Kcal per serve: 670

Ingredients

- 1lb.(450gr) Saku Bar (raw tuna)
- 2 cups Cherry Tomatoes
- 1 cup Extra-Virgin Olive Oil
- 1 cup Mozzarella Cheese, torn into bite-size pieces
- 1 tablespoon Pink Peppercorns
- 1 tablespoon Balsamic vinegar handful Fresh Basil Leaves
- Salt, to taste

Preparation

1. Combine the tuna, cherry tomatoes, pink peppercorns, and olive oil inside the pot. Cook on slow cooker mode set to low for 4 hours.

2. Take the tomatoes and tuna out of the pot. Flake the tuna into bite-sized pieces. Set aside.

3. Take about 3 tablespoons of the olive oil from the pot. Whisk it together with the balsamic vinegar in a salad bowl.

4. Toss in the tuna, tomatoes, basil leaves, and mozzarella.

5. Season with salt.

Cooking tips

Though complete and excellent as this salad already is, feel free to toss your favorite greens, grains, nuts, or fruits in... you've got lots of flavored poaching oil sitting in the pot for mixing up a bigger batch of vinaigrette anyways!

Pork Recipes

||||||||||||||||||||||||||||||||||||||||||||||||||||||||||||||||

Mexican style pork stuffed bell peppers

You will love this quick and easy taste of Mexico. Serve these deliciously spicy bell peppers with diced avocado, sour cream, cilantro and a Mexican-style chunky salsa. For extra indulgence top with shredded pepper jack cheese and broil until the cheese is bubbling and golden brown.

Details

Preparation Time: 15 minutes

Cooking Time: 27 minutes (includes steam release time)

Serves: 2

Kcal per Serve: 800

Ingredients

- 1 can (15oz.) black beans, drained and rinsed
- 4 large red or yellow bell peppers, tops and seeds removed
- ½ lb. lean ground pork
- 1 cup tomato, diced
- 1 small red onion, diced
- 1 jalapeño pepper, deseeded and diced
- ¼ cup cilantro, chopped
- 1 tsp. cumin
- 1 tsp. chili powder, or to taste
- 1 tsp. garlic powder
- 1 tsp. black pepper, or to taste
- 1 tsp. salt, or to taste
- ⅓ cup panko bread crumbs
- 1 ⅓ cups cooked rice
- 1 cup water

Preparation

1. Puree ½ the beans with a stick hand blender or food processor.

2. Add the pureed beans and the remaining ingredients (except the bell peppers and water) to a large bowl and mix together. Stuff the peppers tightly with the pork mixture.3. Place the steam trivet and a cup of water into the Instant Pot.

4. Arrange the bell peppers on the trivet and secure the lid. Set the Instant Pot to Steam for 12 minutes. When done allow the steam to release naturally for 15 minutes before manually releasing the remaining pressure.

Cooking tips

You can use 6 medium bell peppers instead of 4 large bell peppers if your Instant Pot is large enough. If you prefer a meatier stuffed pepper double the ground pork and skip the cooked rice. This recipe also works well with ground beef, chicken or turkey.

Honey & mustard pork chops

These honey and mustard chops are quick and easy to prepare. Rib chops are juicy and tender, and they are perfectly complemented by the savory and sweet flavors of the mustard and honey, with a hint of smokiness from the paprika.

Details

Preparation Time: 10 min.

Cooking Time: 15 minutes

Serves: 2

Kcal per serve: 510

Ingredients

- 4 pork rib chops, bone-in approx. 1 ½" thick (approx. 6 oz.)
- salt & black pepper, to taste
- 2 tbsp. canola or olive oil
- 1 red onion, halved and thinly sliced
- 3 cloves garlic, finely chopped
- 2 tsp. sweet or spicy smoked paprika
- ¼ cup honey
- 2 tsp. Dijon mustard
- 1 tsp. wholegrain mustard
- zest of ⅓ orange
- 2 tbsp. orange juice
- ⅓ cup veal or chicken stock
- 1 tbsp. Worcestershire sauce

Preparation

1. Season the pork chops with salt and black pepper to taste.

2. Set the instant pot to Sauté (more/high) and add the oil. When hot brown the chops, one or two at a time, on both sides for about 1 ½ minutes. Set aside the chops in a bowl.

3. Select Sauté (less), add the onions and cook until soft. Add the garlic and cook for a further minute. Switch the Instant Pot off.

4. Return the chops and any resting juices to the pot.

5. Add the remaining ingredients to a bowl and stir to combine. Pour the mixture over the chops.

6. Secure the lid and set to Manual (more/high) for 1 minute. When done allow the pressure to release naturally.

7. Remove the chops to a warm serving dish. Taste the sauce and adjust the seasoning with salt and pepper if desired. Pour the sauce over the chops.

Cooking tips

If the sauce is too thin dissolve a tablespoon of cornstarch in a little water. Set the pot to Sauté (More/High). When hot stir in the cornstarch a little at a time until you have the desired thickness.

Pork carnitas

Bring a taste of Mexico to the dinner table with this easy to prepare and tasty pulled pork dish. Serve it with a variety of side dishes such as red onion, cilantro, lime wedges, queso fresco and corn tortillas or tacos. It's also perfect for burritos or tossed with a tomato and corn green salad.

Details

Preparation Time: 10 minutes

Cooking Time: 1 hour

Serves: 6

Kcal per serve: 740

Ingredients

- 3 lb. pork shoulder, cut into 6 pieces
- salt and black pepper
- 2 tbsp. olive oil
- 2 cups chicken stock
- 1 large jalapeño pepper, deseeded and chopped
- 1 green bell pepper, deseeded and chopped
- 20 mini tomatoes (1lb), de-husked and quartered
- 1 large red onion, chopped
- 4 cloves garlic, minced
- 1 pepper, de-stalked
- 1 tbsp. ancho chili powder, or to taste
- 1 tsp. ground cumin
- 1 tsp. ground coriander
- 1 tsp. oregano
- 2 bay leaves

Preparation

1. Season the pork shoulder well with salt and black pepper. Set the Instant Pot to Sauté (More/High), add the oil and when hot sauté the pork pieces, in batches, until browned all over.

2. Add the browned pork pieces and all the remaining ingredients to the pot and stir to combine. Set the Instant Pot to Manual (More/High) for 55 minutes. When done naturally release the pressure for 10 minutes before doing a quick release of the remaining pressure.

3. Remove the pork pieces to a baking pan.

4. Set the Instant Pot to Sauté (More/High) and reduce the sauce by half, stirring occasionally.

5. Whilst the sauce is reducing shred the meat using 2 forks.

6. Puree the sauce in the pot with a hand stick blender or in a table blender.

7. Pre-heat the broiler to maximum.

8. Ladle just enough sauce over the meat to moisten. Stir in and spread the meat evenly over the baking pan. Place the pan close to the broiler and broil until the meat is crisp and nicely browned.

9. Serve with the remaining sauce.

Cooking tips

If fresh tomatillos are not available, you can use an 11oz. can as a substitute. If you prefer not to crisp the carnitas skip steps 7 and 8. If you like it extra spicy add more jalapeño and ancho or any chili of choice such as chipotle chili or cayenne.

Pork sausage with bell peppers & basil

This is comfort food at its best especially if served with rich and creamy mashed potatoes or lightly crushed boiled potatoes flavored with Parmesan cheese, parsley, black pepper and butter. It's a simple, rustic dish but using the best quality lean pork sausages you can buy will make all the difference to the result.

Details

Preparation Time: 15 minutes

Cooking Time: 40 minutes

Serves: 4

Kcal per serve: 980

Ingredients

• 12 Italian pork sausages, or sausages of choice (approx. 2.2 lb.)
• 2 tbsp. olive oil
• 1 large onion, halved and sliced
• 3 cloves garlic, thinly sliced
• 1 red bell pepper, deseeded & sliced lengthways into 8 strips
• 1 yellow bell pepper, deseeded & sliced lengthways into 8 strips
• 1 green bell pepper, deseeded & sliced lengthways into 8 strips
• 1 can (28oz.) diced tomatoes
• 1 can (15oz.) Italian tomato sauce of choice
• 1 cup chicken stock or water
• 1 tbsp. Italian herb seasoning
• 1 small bunch basil, sliced

Preparation

1. Set the instant pot to Sauté (more/high). Sauté the sausages, in batches, until nicely browned. Set aside in a bowl.

2. Set to Sauté (less) and add the onions. Sauté for a few minutes until softened. Add the garlic and bell peppers and sauté for 3 minutes. Add the diced tomatoes, Italian tomato sauce, stock, Italian herb seasoning and season with salt and black pepper to taste.

3. Return the sausages to the pot and gently stir so that the sausages are covered with the sauce. Set to Manual (more/high) for 25 minutes. When done release the pressure and remove the lid.

4. Add the basil and gently stir into the sauce.

Cooking tips

If mini bell peppers are available use them instead of the larger ones as they have a sweeter, milder taste. Use 10 - 12 mini peppers (depending on size) of a variety of colors. Simply slice in half, remove the stalk and deseed them.

Pork baby back ribs

What's better than a deliciously sweet and sticky rack of ribs with tender meat almost falling off the bone! If you prepare the ribs ahead of time you will have a great ready-to-grill addition to the summer barbeque menu. And you can use the sauce on other meats too.

Details

Preparation Time: 15 minutes

Cooking Time: 1 hour

Serves: 4

Kcal per serve: 975

Ingredients

- 1 rack (1 ½ lb.) baby back ribs Rub
- 1 tbsp. muscovado sugar
- 2 tsp. black pepper
- 2 tsp. chipotle chili powder, or to taste
- 1 tsp. onion powder
- 1 tsp. garlic powder
- 1 tsp. salt
- 1 tsp. cinnamon powder
- 1 tsp. fennel seed powder
- ½ tsp. ginger powder
- 2 tsp. smoked picante paprika Sauce
- 1 medium red onion, minced
- 3 cloves garlic, minced
- 1 cup tomato ketchup
- ¼ cup maple syrup
- 1 tbsp. muscovado or brown sugar
- 2 tbsp. apple cider or sherry vinegar
- 2 tbsp. Dijon mustard
- ½ cup orange juice or water

Preparation

1. Combine all the rub ingredients together. Rub the rack of ribs on both sides with the spice mix. Set aside.

2. Add all the sauce ingredients to the Instant Pot and stir to combine.

3. Place the ribs into the pot pushing the rack into the sauce. If desired, you can cut the rack in half.

4. Set the instant pot to manual (more/high) for 20 minutes. When done naturally release the pressure.

5. Remove the ribs to a chopping board and cover with aluminum foil.

6. Pre-heat the oven to 450 ºF.

7. Set the pot to Sauté (less) and simmer the sauce for 5 – 7 minutes or until the sauce has reduced and thickened.

8. Slice the rack into individual ribs and place into a baking dish. Pour over the sauce and coat the ribs.

9. Place in the ribs in the oven, near the top, and bake for 10 minutes.

Cooking tips

You can double the quantity of ribs without increasing the amount of sauce. Alternative to using the oven is to finish the ribs on a barbeque grill. Turn and brush the ribs a few times with the sauce.

Smoky butternut squash casserole

Crisped bacon bits, sweet maple syrup, fragrant vanilla extract... all the goodness that reminds you of a slow cooked BBQ feast. That combined with the natural sweetness and velvety smoothness of butternut squash and we've got a truly outstanding vegetable casserole. Would the obvious health benefits of this dish still be worth mentioning?

Details

Preparation Time: 10 minutes

Cooking time: 4 minutes

Serves: 2

Kcal per serve: 500

Ingredients

- 2lb (900gr) Butternut Squash, cut into 1" cubes
- 1/3 lb.(150gr) Bacon, chopped
- 1 White Onion, minced
- 2 tablespoons Maple Syrup
- 1 teaspoon Vanilla Extract
- 1 teaspoon Liquid Smoke
- 2-3 sprigs Fresh Thyme
- 1 cup Chicken Stock
- 1 tablespoon Olive Oil Salt, to taste
- Pepper, to taste

Preparation

1. Set pot to sauté mode.

2. Heat olive oil.

3. Sauté bacon bits until slightly brown.

4. Add chopped onions and sweat until translucent.

5. Pour chicken stock into the pot and scrape any pan drippings loose.

6. Add the chopped squash, maple syrup, vanilla extract, liquid smoke, and fresh thyme.

7. Cook for high pressure for 4 minutes. Release pressure.

8. Season with salt and pepper if needed.

Cooking tips

Bacon may be skipped, and vegetable stock used for a totally vegetarian take on this dish. Otherwise, Spanish chorizo may be added for an even smokier flavor profile.

Ma po tofu

Fermented black beans and chili paste team up effectively to give this humble Sichuan tofu dish that perfect balance of tang, heat, and flavor. Furthermore, this dish showcases contrasting textures like no other – perfectly moist meat mince, springy shiitake mushrooms, silky smooth tofu, and crisp roasted peanuts. Those taste buds are in for a big surprise!

Details

Prep time: 20 minutes

Cooking time: 30 minutes

Serves: 2

Kcal per serve: 800

Ingredients

- 1/2 lb.(225 gr) Minced Pork
- 1 block Silken Tofu (approx. 1lb or 450 gr), cut into inch cubes
- 1 cup Shiitake Mushrooms, sliced ½ cup Chicken Broth
- 2 tbsp. Chili Bean Paste
- 2 tbsp. Fermented Black Beans, roughly chopped
- 6 cloves Garlic, minced
- 1 tbsp. Ginger, minced
- 1 tsp. Sichuan Peppercorns
- 2 tsp. Low Sodium Soy Sauce
- 1 tbsp. Sesame Oil
- 1 tbsp. Chili Oil
- 1 tbsp. Vegetable Oil
- 1 tsp. Sugar
- 4 stalks Green Onion, thinly sliced
- ¼ cup Roasted Peanuts, roughly chopped
- 1 teaspoon Cornstarch, dissolved in 1 teaspoon water

Preparation

1. Set pot to sauté mode and heat vegetable oil.

2. Sauté pork until brown.

3. Add garlic, ginger, and Sichuan peppercorns. Sauté until aromatic.

4. Add shiitake, chili bean paste, fermented black beans, chicken broth, soy sauce, and sugar. Simmer for 5 minutes.

5. Stir in cornstarch slurry. Leave for 2-3 minutes to thicken.

6. Add silken tofu and leave for a few minutes to get warm.

7. Top with sesame oil, chili oil, green onions, and chopped peanuts before serving.

Cooking tips

Make your own version of Ma Po Tofu, adding in chicken, seafood, or any other protein of your choice. An assortment of mushrooms would work well for a completely vegetarian take on this classic.

Instant pot pork luau

It's the same Kalua Pork... succulent, tender, and smoky, less all the hassle of having to dig up a deep roasting pit. The slow cooker mode of your instant pot surprisingly does a really good job in the recreation of this Hawaiian favorite!

Details

Preparation Time: 5 minutes

Cooking time: 4 hours

Serves: 2

Kcal per serve: 600

Ingredients

- 2lb. (900gr) Pork Shoulder, skin removed
- 2 tablespoons Liquid Smoke
- 1 tablespoon Coarse Salt

Preparation

1. Rub salt and liquid smoke all over the pork shoulder.

2. Set inside the pot, fat-side up.

3. Cook on slow cooker mode set to high for 4 hours. Release pressure.

4. Take the pork out of the pot and shred apart.

5. Take some of the cooking liquid in the pot and ladle onto the pulled pork meat.

Cooking tips

When possible, try wrapping the pork in real banana leaves inside the pot. You'll be amazed how it'll end up smokier, more flavorful, and closer to the real thing!

Deonjang pork spare ribs

Bone-in cuts of pork and fermented soy bean paste combine in this exceptionally umami-rich Korean-inspired dish. Apples, soy sauce, sesame, and a few other choice aromatics only add further complexity. An easy all-in-one-pot meal that yields a depth of flavor that really is quite hard to match.

Details

Preparation Time: 5 minutes

Cooking time: 20-25 minutes

Serves: 4

Kcal per serve: 730

Ingredients

- 1.5 Kg (3.5lb.) Pork Spare Ribs
- 1 White Onion, peeled and quartered
- 2 Scallions, cut into 2" pieces
- 6 cloves Garlic
- crushed thumb-sized piece Ginger, thinly sliced
- 1 cup Pork Stock
- 3 tbsp. Soy Sauce
- 3 tbsp. Mirin
- 2 tbsp. Honey
- 1 tbsp. Sesame Oil
- 2 tbsp. Gochujang (or substitute)*
*Substitute: Chili peppers +Soya sauce +Sugar
- 1 small Apple, grated
- 1 tbsp. Sesame Seeds

Preparation

1. Combine stock, soy sauce, mirin, honey, sesame oil, gochujang, deonjang, apples, and sesame seeds in a blender. Process until smooth.

2. Arrange the pork ribs, onions, scallions, garlic, and ginger inside the pot.

3. Pour the blended sauce over the pork and cook on high pressure for 20-25 minutes. Release pressure.

Cooking tips

Spare ribs are ideal for the extra depth of flavor made possible by using bone-in cuts of meat. Beef ribs or chicken thighs would be perfect substitutions.

Caribbean pulled pork salad

||||||||||||||||||||||||||||||||||||||||||||||||||||||||||||||||||||||||||||||||||||||||||||||||||||||

A festive dish that truly captures the vibrant flavors of the Tropics. Oranges, pineapples, avocados, and a mix of interesting island spices make this pork dish like no other.

Details

Preparation Time: 30 minutes

Cooking time: 4 hours

Serves: 4

Kcal per serve: 740

Ingredients

- 2lb. (900gr) Pork Shoulder

For the Salad
- 3 Oranges, cut into segments
- 2 Avocados, cut into cubes
- 6 cups Baby Spinach Leaves
- 2 Red Bell Peppers
- ½ cup Golden Raisins
- 4 cups thinly sliced Napa Cabbage

For the Marinade
- 6 cloves Garlic, crushed
- ¼ cup Brown Sugar
- 1 teaspoon Ground Allspice
- 1 teaspoon Salt
- 1 teaspoon Black Pepper
- ¼ teaspoon Ground Cinnamon
- ¼ teaspoon Ground Cumin
- ¼ teaspoon Ground Cloves
- juice of 2 Limes
- juice of 1 Orange
- 1 cup Pineapple chunks
- 2 Red Onions, chopped
- a bunch of Cilantro, roughly chopped

Preparation

1. Combine all ingredients for the marinade in a blender. Pulse into a smooth paste.

2. Stab the pork shoulder all over with a pairing knife.

3. Pour the marinade all over the pork and leave to marinate overnight in the chiller.

4. Put the pork and marinade into the pot.

5. Set pot to slow cooker mode set to high and leave for 4 hours. Release pressure.

6. Take the pork out of the pot and shred with 2 forks.

7. Combine the salad components with some of the cooking stock in a bowl and toss well.

8. Serve the pulled pork with the prepared salad on the side.

Cooking tips

It'll be worth making a big batch of this jerk marinade. Use it for chicken, beef, turkey, lamb... it really was meant to flavor any type of meat!

Easy egg and cheese bacon strata

An easy to make breakfast, recommended for both adults and children. It is so simple to make that you may get your children helping. It is perfect for getting rid of stale French bread and is so adaptable you easily can change the ingredients. You may combine two or three hard cheeses rather than using just the aged cheddar.

Details

Prep time: 20 minutes

Cooking time: 30 minutes

Serves: 4

Kcal per serve: 880

Ingredients

- 6 cups of cubed French bread
- 1 cup of cooked bacon pieces
- ½ cup of chopped celery
- 10 free-range eggs
- 2 cups of milk, semi-skimmed
- 1 1/2 cups of shredded aged cheddar
- 1 tsp. of ground black pepper
- 1 tsp. of garlic powder
- 1 tsp. of onion powder
- 1 tsp. of natural chicken seasoning
- 1/2 tsp. of ground cayenne pepper

Preparation

1. Cut your stale French bread into 1 or 2-inch cubes. If you have French bread, toast them up first so the bread will harden and become crumblier. In this way, when you mix them with the wet ingredients, they will quickly absorb the moisture like a sponge.

2. Prepare your bacon pieces. If you are using fresh bacon strips, chop them into small bits and cook them up first. If you are using store-bought crumbled bacon, simply open the package and pour the content to fill 1 measuring cup.

3. Chop your celery to fill half a cup.

4. Grate your aged cheddar to fit one and a half cups. If you are using store-bought shredded cheddar, cut open the package and measure according to the ingredient list.

5. Break open and whisk the free-range eggs in a large bowl along with two cups of milk, ground black pepper, garlic powder, onion powder, natural chicken seasoning and cayenne pepper.

6. Prepare another large mixing bowl. Dump the cubed bread, bacon pieces, chopped celery, and 1 cup of cheddar cheese. Mix using a large salad fork or spatula until the celery and cheese are distributed evenly.

7. Add the egg mixture into the bread bowl. Mix them up. The mixture should be wet but not too watery either. The bread should absorb most of the egg mixture.

8. Set the trivet inside the Instant Pot and add water.

9. Lightly grease a baking or springform pan. Pour the bread mixture inside. Cover with aluminum foil.

10. Set the baking pan on the trivet. Lock the lid and cook on manual for 20 minutes.

11. Let the pressure release naturally.

12. Top with the remaining cheese and gratinate in the broiler.

Honey and garlic pork roast with baked beans and sour cream

A dish adding sourness and garlic to the usual slow cooker preparation of pork roast shoulder. Marinate the pork with chili garlic sauce and honey to give this dish both hot and sweet tastes at once. Baked beans and roasted sesame seeds provide extra flavor and crunch.

Details

Prep time: 20 minutes

Cooking time: 20 minutes

Serves: 3

Kcal per serve: 650

Ingredients

- 2 lb. boneless pork shoulder roast
- 2 tablespoons honey
- 2 tablespoons sesame seeds
- 2 tablespoons chili garlic sauce
- Salt and black pepper, as per taste
- 1 can baked beans
- 1 cup sun dried tomatoes
- 8-10 cloves garlic, finely chopped
- 1 medium onion, diced
- 8-10 button mushrooms, sliced
- 1 cup chicken broth
- 2 tablespoons sour cream

Preparation

1. Wash and pat dry the pork. Take a large mixing bowl and combine the honey, sesame seeds, chili garlic sauce along with some salt and pepper. Rub the mixture all over the pork. Place the pork in the refrigerator for 30 minutes.

2. After half an hour, pour some olive oil in the Instant Pot and place the pork in.

3. Add the baked beans, tomatoes, garlic, onions, and mushrooms. Pour some chicken broth along with sour cream and stir every well.

4. Sprinkle some salt and pepper.

5. Close the lid and cook for 20-25 minutes on high pressure.

6. Let the pressure release naturally.

Cooking tips

Roast your pork with herbs such as basil, thyme, and oregano to provide additional aroma and freshness. Add vinegar and white wine near the end of the cooking time, when the pork is nearly done.

Mashed beans with sun-dried tomatoes, bacon and ham

A mashed beans recipe displaying sundried tomatoes, ham and bacon offers a practical alternative to the traditional Tex-Mex or Mexican refried beans. Rather than boiling beans for one hour and then finishing in a sauté pan; sauté the bacon, ham and onions in a pan to start and then finish it all in the pressure cooker.

Details

Prep Time using beans: 15 minutes

Prep Time using dried beans: 45 minutes

Cooking Time: 30 minutes

Serves: 4

Kcal per serve: 920

Ingredients

- 3 cups of fresh pinto beans
- 1 cup of sun-dried tomatoes
- ½ cup of chopped red bell peppers
- 6 cups of chicken stock
- 1 cup of diced ham
- 1 cup of bacon, cut into pieces
- 1 cup of chopped onion
- 1 tbsp. of olive oil
- 1 tbsp. of coarse sea salt
- 1 tsp. of ground black pepper
- 1 tsp. of ground cumin

Preparation

1. Wash and drain the pinto beans. If you are using the dried beans, soak them for at least 30 minutes and rinse in cold water to remove dried dirt or debris that may stick on the surface. If you are using canned pinto beans, simply open the can and drain the liquid. Directly go to the next step.

2. Open your canned sun-dried tomatoes. Drain the tomatoes of the liquid. You should have 1 cup of sun-dried tomatoes (without the canning liquid).

3. Peel and dice your onions to make 1 cup of diced onions.

4. Cut the strips of bacon into small square bits, approximately 1-cm. This way, they will lend their meaty aroma to the recipe and still maintain their chewy texture. Dice the ham to make 1x1 inch cubes.

5. Set the instant pot to sauté.

6. Heat olive oil and sauté onions until fragrant. Add the cubed ham and bacon pieces. Sauté for about 2-3 minutes or until the onions, ham and bacon become fragrant. You should see changes in color and texture of the bacon by this time.

7. Add the pinto beans, sun-dried tomatoes, chicken stock, salt, pepper, and cumin.

8. Lock the lid and cook on high pressure for 30 minutes.

9. Let the pressure release naturally then mash the bean mixture using a potato masher.

Pineapple and pepper Hawaiian pork

An essential meal for those cold and wet days in winter. The Pineapple's sweetness will bring you back to sunny summertime days by the beach. This dish is simple to prepare and very adaptable. Lacking pork loin, other pork products may be used, such as pork sausages, bacon or even SPAM. A great way to add fibre and fruit to your diet.

Details

Prep Time: 10-20 minutes

Cooking Time: 15 minutes

Serves:

Kcal per serve: 710

Ingredients

- 14 oz (400 gr) of pork loin roast
- 2 cups of diced pineapples
- ½ cup of sweet bell peppers (red)
- ½ cup of sweet bell peppers (yellow)
- ½ cup of sweet yellow onions
- 1 cup of pineapple juice
- 1 cup of water
- ½ tsp. salt
- ¼ tsp. pepper (or to taste)

Preparation

1. Peel and cut the pineapples into 2-inch chunks (slightly larger than bite-sized pieces) to fill two measuring cups.

2. Wash and drain your peppers and onions. Deseed the peppers and remove the stem. Chop into large chunks approximately the same width as the pineapples. Do the same thing with the onions.

3. Cut the pork loin into thin strips, approximately 1-inch thick each. Sprinkle some salt and pepper.

4. Combine all ingredients in the Instant Pot.

5. Cook on high pressure for 15 minutes.

6. Quick-release the pressure.

7. Open the lid and add the pineapples. Simmer for 5 more minutes.

Cooking tips

Make this recipe more flavorful by adding a quarter-cup of crumbled bacon. You may alter the recipe and utilize whole pork loin roast. Bacon strips on top will provide a strong umami flavor. Use 200 grams of chicken breast (cubed) or turkey instead of the pork loin roast to make a leaner recipe.

Pork chops with sweet and savory apple sauce

Featuring pork chops with a tasty and sweet apple sauce, you have found here a simple recipe to make. It is difficult to do much wrong with just onions, apples and pork. Include some of your favourite spices and it will turn out terrific. You may even buy a spice mix from the grocery store and no one will notice the difference. Wonderful for weekends when you don't feel like cooking, but relatives or friends are on the way over.

Details

Prep Time: 20-30 minutes

Cooking Time: 20 minutes

Serves: 4

Kcal per serve: 580

Ingredients

- 3 large-sized pork chops (8 oz. each)
- 500 grams of chopped apples (17.6 oz)
- 1 tablespoon butter
- 2 tablespoons brown sugar
- 2 tablespoons minced garlic
- ½ teaspoon thyme
- 1 cup of chopped onions
- 1 cup of chicken broth
- 2 tablespoons of red wine vinegar
- Pinch of salt and pepper

Preparation

1. Peel and cut out the cores of the apples. Remove the seeds. You can either cut the apples into sections or cut the apples into 0.5 or 1-inch cubes. Peel and mince the garlic. Peel and chop the onions into quarters. Chop the fresh thyme.

2. In a bowl, mix the chicken broth, brown sugar, red wine, thyme, salt, and black pepper.

3. Set the instant pot to sauté and heat the butter.

4. Season the pork chops with salt and pepper on both sides.

5. Add the pork chops into the pot and sear on both sides until a crust appears.

6. Add the apples, onions, and seasoning liquid mixture.

7. Close the lid and cook on high pressure for 15-20 minutes.

8. Release the pressure naturally.

9. Serve the pork chops according to your preferred serving portions on individual serving plates and ladle the sauce over the meat.

Cooking tips

Make your sauce more savory by adding a pinch of chicken seasoning mix during the cooking. Make it sweeter and more caramelized by adding one tablespoon of raisins and a pinch of ground clover. This dish is rather adaptable for other red meats. You may replace by lamb, venison or beef for the pork.

Pork loin roast with caramelized onions and balsamic vinegar

This pork loin roast makes a wonderful main dish for virtually any occasion or celebration. Pork loin roasts are not difficult to portion since they often are sold in one-pound packages. It is so adaptable that any number of seasonings can be added: garlic, thyme and rosemary for an Italian roast or dark and light soy sauce and five-spice powder for Chinese roast.

Details

Prep Time: 25-30 minutes

Cooking Time: 30 minutes

Serves: 2

Kcal per serve: 560

Ingredients

- 14.0 oz (400gr) boneless pork loin roast (2 large slabs of tenderloin, 7.0 oz or 200 gr each
- 3 large sweet yellow onions
- 4 cloves of garlic, crushed
- 2 cloves of garlic, pressed
- 1/4 cup of Balsamic vinegar
- ½ cup of Worcestershire sauce
- 1 cup of water
- 1 tbsp. of ketchup (tomato sauce)
- 1 tbsp. of hot sauce (optional)
- 2 tbsps. of Olive Oil
- 1 tsp. of Garlic salt
- Pinch of sea salt
- Ground black pepper

Preparation

1. Peel the onion. Cut each into two lengthwise. If you plan to caramelize them, julienne to half-inch thickness. If dumping all ingredients altogether into the pan, cut into large cubes and do not break the sections.

2. In a bowl, make the sauce mixture. Mix together the Balsamic vinegar, Worcestershire sauce, ketchup, hot sauce, water, and a pinch of salt and ground black pepper.

3. Crush 4 cloves of garlic using the back of a knife.

4. Take your pork loins. Cut some fat tissues that are still left on the surface. Pat them dry with a kitchen towel. Take some garlic salt and ground black pepper. Rub the garlic salt on the tenderloin roast. Then, cut slits on the top and bottom side of the pork loin roast. Do not cut through.

5. Line the bottom of the Instant Pot with the onions. Place the pork loin roast on top. Pour the vinegar mixture and crushed garlic on top. Flip the tenderloin several times to make sure all sides are coated with the seasoning mixture.

6. Lock the lid and cook on high pressure for 30 minutes.

7. Release the pressure naturally.

8. Take the pork loin and leave it to rest for 15 minutes before cutting.

9. Serve drizzled with the cooking sauce and caramelized onions, alongside warm side dishes.

Soup & Stew Recipes

||||||||||||||||||||||||||||||||||||||||||||||||||

Beef ribs, kidney beans, and root vegetables stew

A delicious stew including root vegetables, kidney beans and beef. A wonderful choice for using less expensive meat. The ribs provide the beef broth with a stronger, deeper, more savoury aroma. The beef flavour is balanced with the addition of bay leaves, nutmeg, clove and a half teaspoon of ground coffee. The green onions, shallots and garlic are sautéd, adding a richer taste.

Details

Prep Time: 25-30 minutes

Cooking Time: 40 minutes

Serves: 3

Kcal per serve: 820

Ingredients

- 14.0 oz (400gr) beef ribs, trimmed to ¼ inch
- 1 cup of raw, red kidney beans
- 1 ½ cup of carrots
- 1 ½ cup of potatoes
- 1 ½ cup of crushed diced tomatoes
- 4 cups of beef broth
- ¼ teaspoon of ground clove
- ½ teaspoon of grated nutmeg
- ½ tsp of ground Arabica coffee beans
- 1 tablespoon of rock sugar
- 1 tablespoon of garlic
- ½ cup of shallots, 2 bay leaves
- 1 cup of green onions
- 2 tablespoons of coconut oil
- ½ tsp of ground cayenne pepper
- Salt and pepper to taste

Preparation

1. Ask your butcher to cut the beef ribs into individual sections. Wash, peel and chop carrots and potatoes to 1-inch thickness. Rinse and drain the kidney beans. Grate the nutmeg; grind the Arabica coffee beans and clove. Chop the green onions to fill 1 cup. Peel and chop the shallots to fill half a measuring cup. Peel and mince the garlic. Open the canned crushed, diced tomatoes and fill one and a half measuring cups.

2. Heat coconut oil in the instant pot.

3. Sauté the shallots, green onions, and garlic until shallots turn translucent with caramelized edges and the green onions have some browned spots.

4. Add the beef ribs, red kidney beans, crushed diced tomatoes, beef broth, ground cloves, ground nutmeg, ground coffee beans, rock sugar, and bay leaves.

5. Lock the lid and cook on manual for 30 minutes.

6. Quick-release the pressure and add the chopped carrots and chopped potatoes. Simmer for 10 minutes or until vegetables are cooked al dente.

7. Add salt and pepper to taste.

Cooking tips

You may use other meat, such beef ribeye or beef loin, instead of the beef ribs. Even pork, lamb or venison will work perfectly in this dish. To make it in the oven, follow the first two steps, preheating to 350 degrees, and leave for 45 minutes to one hour.

Creamy corn and asparagus chicken soup

This savoury and sweet asparagus and creamy corn chicken soup uses chicken breast chunks cooked slowly in creamed corn with chunks of asparagus. Beaten eggs provide a silky-smooth texture. Dehydrated carrots or mushrooms can be included for additional fibre. Top it off with caramelized onions or chopped scallions for a stronger umami flavour.

Details

Prep Time: 15-20 minutes

Cooking Time: 40 minutes

Serves: 4

Kcal per serve: 920

Ingredients

- 14oz (400 gr) of chicken breast, diced
- 2 cups of canned corn, cream style
- 1 cup of corn, frozen
- 1 cup of canned asparagus, chopped
- 2 cups of chicken broth
- 2 tbsps. cornstarch
- 2 tbsps. garlic
- 1 tbsp. grated ginger root
- ¼ cup of onions, minced
- 1 tsp. white pepper
- 3 tbsps. oyster sauce
- 1 tbsp. light soy sauce
- ½ tbsp. salt
- 2 eggs, beaten

Preparation

1. Dice the chicken breast into bite-sized pieces. They will shrink a bit during cooking but that is okay.

2. Open the canned corn and asparagus. Chop the asparagus roughly to 2-inch sticks.

3. Dilute the cornstarch with two tablespoons of the chicken broth. After this, peel and grate the ginger using a microplane grater to get one tablespoonful of grated ginger root. You may use ground ginger if you do not have fresh ginger.

4. In a small bowl, crack the egg, add one tablespoon of oyster sauce. Beat the eggs with a fork until the oyster sauce is well-combined into the egg.

5. Combine the cream style corn, asparagus, chicken breast, chicken broth, garlic, grated ginger root, onions, white pepper, oyster sauce, salt, and light soy sauce in the Instant Pot.

6. Cook on manual for 10 minutes. Release pressure naturally.

7. Stir in the cornstarch slurry and simmer until thick.

8. Add the beaten eggs, stir, and continue to simmer until eggs are set.

9. Before serving, add your preferred toppings but this step is optional. You may add chopped scallions, toasted sesame and sesame oil, or caramelized onions. These toppings intensify the umami flavor of the soup.

Cooking tips

Make it on the stove: Put together all the ingredients and boil them for forty-five minutes to one hour. Ensure the cubed chicken is well-done and changes color. During the final ten minutes, put in the eggs and stir periodically so they will cook completely.

Irish lamb stew with red wine

A satisfying meal your family will enjoy: It does not require browning the onions, which reduces the calorie count. A variety of meats may be used, including lamb shoulder, lamb shank or the leaner lamb loin. New Zealand lamb is a good choice for texture and taste.

Details

Prep Time: 15-20 minutes

Cooking Time: 30 minutes

Serves: 2

Kcal per serve: 510

Ingredients

- 14 oz (400 gr) of lamb shank or loin
- 2 tbsps. all-purpose flour
- 2 tbsps. garlic, minced
- ½ cup of onions
- 2 cups of vegetable broth
- ½ cup of water
- 1 cup of carrots
- 1 cup of potatoes
- ¼ cup of tomato paste
- ½ cup of red wine
- 1 tsp. thyme
- 1 tsp. rosemary sprig
- 1 bay leaf
- ½ cup celery ribs, chopped
- 1 tsp. ground black pepper
- 1 tsp. of sea salt

Preparation

1. Cut the lamb shank or sirloin to 2-inch cubes. They should be slightly larger than bite-sized pieces because they will shrink during the cooking process.

2. Peel and mince the garlic. Peel and roughly chop the onions. Peel and slice the carrots into two and cut each slice into large 2-inch chunks. Peel and dice the potatoes into large 2-inch cubes. Chop the celery ribs.

3. Heat olive oil in the instant pot.

4. Season the lamb pieces with salt and pepper and dust with flour.

5. Sear the lamb pieces until brown on all sides.

6. Add the onions and garlic. Sauté until aromatic.

7. Add the tomato paste and roast for about a minute.

8. Deglaze the pot with red wine. Let the red wine reduce.

9. Add stock, carrots, potatoes, celery, thyme, rosemary, and bay leaf.

10. Lock the lid and cook on high pressure for 25-30 minutes.

11. Release pressure naturally.

12. Season with salt and pepper.

Cooking tips

Dutch oven: combine the root vegetables, celery, lamb, tomato paste, red wine, vegetable broth, and the remaining aromatics. Cover and bake for two hours in a preheated oven. Rather than vegetable broth, you may use chicken broth, lamb broth or beef broth. Simply ensure you use the low-sodium or homemade version.

Quinoa and Black-eyed beans chicken soup

A simple yet satisfying dish. Loaded with alkaline-inducing vegetables, lean proteins, good carbohydrates, vitamins and minerals, makes it a healthy choice. Reduce the cooking time by using canned beans or frozen mixed vegetables.

Details

Prep Time: 15-20 minutes

Cooking Time: 15 minutes

Serves: 2

Kcal per serve: 700

Ingredients

- 14 oz (400 gr) chicken breast (14.0 oz)
- 3/4 cup of raw, dried, black-eyed beans
- 3/4 cup of corn kernels
- 1 cup of carrots, peeled and chopped
- 1 cup of sweet potatoes, peeled and chopped
- ¾ cup of chopped canned tomatoes
- 3/4 cup of raw quinoa
- 1/3 cup of chopped celery
- ½ cup of onions, diced
- ½ tablespoon garlic, minced
- ½ teaspoon dried oregano
- ½ teaspoon dried chili flakes
- ½ teaspoon sea salt
- ½ teaspoon ground black pepper
- ½ teaspoon chicken bouillon cube

Preparation

1. Prepare the ingredients. Cut the chicken breast into big chunks. Peel and chop the onions. Open the canned chopped tomatoes. Peel and mince the garlic. Peel and chop the carrots and sweet potatoes into slightly bigger than bite-sized chunks. Shred your corn to get ¾ cup of corn kernels. Rinse the dried black-eyed beans and quinoa under cold running water to remove debris or inedible hulls that may be present.

2. Combine all ingredients in the Instant Pot and cook on high pressure for 20 minutes. Release pressure naturally.

3. Shred the chicken with two forks and adjust seasoning as necessary. You may also add more water or stock to thin the soup to your liking.

Cooking tips

Some prefer a smooth-textured soup. If this is the case, use an immersion blender to smooth the cooked vegetables in the soup. Then add the shredded chicken back to the soup.

Smoked Ham and Chicken soup with eggs

||||||||||||||||||||||||||||||||||||||||||||||||||||||||||||||||||||||||||||||||||||||||||||||||||||||||||||||||||||||||||||||||||||

A tasty medley of chicken, vegetables and ham cooked in chicken broth with eggs threaded into it. Add soy sauce and sour cream for additional flavour and enjoy this hearty and mouth-watering soup.

Details

Prep Time: 15-20 minutes

Cooking Time: 15 minutes

Serves: 4

Kcal per serve: 870

Ingredients

- 1 tablespoon olive oil
- 1 large bay leaf
- 7-8 peppercorns, crushed
- 3-4 cloves
- 5 garlic cloves, chopped
- An inch of ginger, peeled and grated
- 1 cup chopped onion
- 1 cup carrots, peeled and chopped
- 3.5 oz (100 gr) French beans, chopped (3.5 oz)
- 7-8 baby corns sliced
- 1 cup celery, sliced
- Salt and white pepper, as per taste
- 17.5 oz (500 gr) smoked ham
- 3-4 cups chicken stock
- 35 oz (1kg) minced chicken
- 3 large eggs
- 1/2 cup light sour cream
- Soy sauce, as per taste

Preparation

1. Heat olive oil in the instant pot.

2. Add bay leaf, cloves, and crushed peppercorns. Roast until aromatic.

3. Sauté the garlic, ginger, and onions.

4. Add the carrots, beans, baby corns, celery, and ham.

5. Pour in the stock and add the minced chicken.

6. Sprinkle in salt and white pepper.

7. Cover and cook on manual for 10-15 minutes. Quick release the pressure in the pot.

8. Crack the eggs into the soup and simmer until eggs are fully cooked.

9. Stir in the soy sauce and sour cream before serving.

Cooking tips

Add baked beans when you add the soy sauce to provide some tangy flavour. Optionally, try adding fresh rosemary and thyme to give the soup a pleasant aroma.

Spicy veggie and tilapia soup

A delicious, healthy and spicy vegetable soup with a significant protein punch, makes use of inexpensive and delicious tilapia. You will not believe it contains less than eighty calories per serving! The protein content not only will keep you full, but the omega-3 oils will maintain your heart healthy. Just chop, add some seasoning, set the Instant Pot and wait. In less than six hours, you will have a meal doing wonders for your waistline.

Details

Prep Time: 20 minutes

Cooking Time: 25 minutes

Serves: 2

Kcal per serve: 825

Ingredients

- 1 lb. Tilapia Filet
- 3 cup chicken broth
- 1 cup raw onion
- 1 cup green pepper
- 5 cup brown rice
- 4 garlic cloves, chopped
- 1 can diced tomatoes with celery
- 1 Tbs ground cumin
- 2 Tbs chilli powder
- 1 Tbs Salt
- Pepper to taste
- 1 cup chopped cherry tomatoes
- 1 cup carrots
- 1 cup chopped fresh cilantro
- .5 cup fresh corn

Preparation

1. Combine all ingredients in the instant pot.

2. Cover and cook on manual for 25 minutes.

3. Release the pressure naturally.

4. Serve with hot sauce, sour cream, and cilantro.

Chicken, tofu and mixed vegetables clear Soup

|||||||||||||||||||||||||||||||||||||||||||||||||||||||||||||||||||||||||||||||||||||||||||||||||||||||||||

A clear soup that is easy and quick for those cutting back on their dairy. No need to puree any ingredients or adding any cream. Make it vegetarian by removing chicken and using vegetable broth.

Details

Prep time: 25-30 minutes

Cooking time: 30minutes

Serves: 4

Kcal per serve: 680

Ingredients

- 14 oz (400 gr) boneless, skinless chicken thigh
- 1 cup of fresh black ear fungus
- 4 cups of frozen mix vegetables: (carrots, beans, peas, sweet corn)
- 1 package of firm block tofu
- 3 cloves of garlic
- 3 tbsps. chopped celery
- 1 tbsp. of salt
- ½ tsp. of ground white pepper
- 5 cups of chicken stock
- 2 tbsps. olive oil
- 2 tbsps. oyster sauce
- 1 tsp. sesame oil

Preparation

1. Peel and chop your garlic. Grind the white peppercorns. Hydrate the black ear fungus by soaking them in warm water. Let the fungus sit and bloom for 10-15 minutes. In the meantime, chop the celery to make 3 tablespoons of celery.

2. Cut the boneless, skinless chicken thigh to bite-sized pieces or slightly larger according to personal preference (approximately 1.5-2 inch long). Sprinkle with salt and a bit of white pepper. Set aside.

3. Divide the firm block tofu into two. Cut each block into 1-2 inch dices. Pan sear them on a nonstick pan over medium heat with 1 tbsp. of olive oil until streaks of golden brown crusts appear. It takes approximately 3-4 minutes to pan sear the cubed tofu. Set the pan seared tofu aside.

4. Once the black ear fungus is hydrated cut the stalk and separate or chop the ears into bite-sized pieces.

5. Heat some olive oil in the Instant Pot.

6. Sear the chicken pieces until the pink meat starts to change color.

7. Add the stock, garlic, salt, ground white pepper, and oyster sauce into the pot.

8. Close the lid and cook on high for 25-30 minutes.

9. Release the pressure in the pot manually then add the frozen mixed vegetables, chopped celery, pan-seared tofu cubes, and black ear fungus. Simmer for 5 minutes.

10. Adjust seasoning.

11. Add sesame oil before serving.

Classic beef stew with mushroom and peas

A beef stew recipe using classic ingredients, adding Portobello mushrooms for an interesting twist. The mushrooms provide an exotic flavour and a meaty, chewy texture. Remove the gills with a spoon and slice the outer edge so you can slice it into small cubes. Cook this stew for six to eight hours on low (for creamy texture) or four hours on high.

Details

Prep time: 20-30 minutes

Cooking time: 30min.

Serves: 2

Kcal per serve: 520

Ingredients

- 7 oz (200 gr) of beef loin
- 1 cup of Portobello mushroom
- 1 cup of peeled and cubed potatoes
- 1 cup of carrots
- 1 cup of onions
- 1 cup of cherry tomatoes
- 1 cup of tomato puree
- 2 cups of beef stock
- 2 tbsps. all-purpose flour
- 2 bay leaves
- 1 tsp. dried rosemary
- 1 tsp. of cayenne pepper powder
- Salt and freshly ground black pepper
- 2 tbsps. chopped parsley leaves

Preparation

1. Cut the beef loin into 1 or 2-inch cubes. Set aside in the refrigerator while you prepare the other vegetables. Otherwise, prepare the beef last after you have finished with all of the vegetables.

2. Wash the mushrooms, remove the gills and stem. Cut the tops into 1-inch cubes. Wash and peel your potatoes. Make sure you choose hard potatoes that will not break apart easily.

3. Wash and peel the carrots. Depending on the diameter, cut into 1 or 2-inch logs (the larger the diameter, you need to cut it shorter).

4. Cut the onion into large chunks. If using medium-sized onion, divide it into two and cut each half into quarters.

5. Open the can of the tomato puree or you can make the tomato puree by crushing ripened tomatoes with an immersion blender(or just use your regular blender). Ground your black peppercorns.

6. Slice the cherry tomatoes into two. Wash and chop your parsley leaves to fill two tablespoons. If you don't have any fresh parsley at home, you may use dried parsley flakes. Use 1

tablespoon only or add more according to personal preference.

7. Combine all ingredients except for the parsley in the Instant Pot. Lock the lid and cook on high pressure for 30 minutes. Release pressure naturally.

8. Adjust seasoning to taste and garnish with freshly chopped parsley.

Instant pot beef and red wine stew

There is nothing like a hearty beef stew cooked for hours. Nothing can match its unbelievably tender texture. Every inch is infused with symphony of flavours from the delicious brew. Besides adding bulk to the stew, the vegetables offer depth of flavour while the wine lends sweetness, acidity, complexity and mouth-watering aromatics.

Details

Prep Time: 15 min

Cooking Time: 30min.

Serves: 4

Kcal per serve: 740

Ingredients

- 3 lb. pot roast, trimmed, quartered
- 1 ¼ lbs. carrots, into 1-inch chunks
- 2 cups beef broth, reduced sodium
- 1 cup dry red wine
- ¼ cup tomato sauce
- 5 garlic cloves, peeled, chopped
- 2 ribs of celery, into 1-inch chunks
- 1 large onion, cut into chunks
- 1 tablespoon butter
- 1 tablespoon vegetable oil
- 2 teaspoons soy sauce
- 1 teaspoon dried basil
- Kosher salt
- Black pepper

Preparation

1. Season the pot roast with salt and pepper on all sides.

2. Heat vegetable oil in the Instant Pot set to sear.

3. Sear the pot roast until brown on all sides. Set aside.

4. Add the carrots, onions, and celery into the pot and sweat until onions are translucent.

5. Add the garlic and sauté for another minute.

6. Deglaze the pot with red wine, scraping all burnt bits at the bottom. Let the wine reduce.

7. Add the broth, soy sauce, and dried basil.

8. Put the beef back into the pot.

9. Lock the lid and cook on high pressure for 30 minutes.

10. Release the pressure naturally.

11. Adjust seasoning if needed.

12. Shred the beef and serve.

Cooking tips

Pot roast is a general term used to describe various cuts of meat used in braised beef dishes and stews. The cuts you can use include chuck, brisket, and round. Also, never cook with a wine you would not drink. The flavors of the wine make their way into the stew so if you don't like the wine, you won't like the taste they add to the recipe.

Turkey Recipes

||||||||||||||||||||||||||||||||||||||||||||||||||||

Turkey breast with fennel

||||||||||||||||||||||||||||||||||||||||||||||||||||||||||||||||||||||||||||||||||||||||||||||||||||

Pressured-cooked turkey breast is moist, juicy and delicious. You won't get crispy and golden browned skin as you would with roasting, but this is a great alternative way to serve delicious slices of turkey for a crowd without spending ages in the kitchen. Left-overs are also perfect for sandwiches.

Details

Prep Time: 15 min.

Cooking Time: 35 min.

Serves: 4

Kcal per serve: 700

Ingredients

- 3.5 lb. whole turkey breast, bone-in & skin on
- salt and black pepper to taste
- 1 large onion, diced
- 2 carrots, peeled & diced
- 2 stick celery, diced
- 2 cloves garlic, minced
- 1 bulb fennel, root removed, halved and sliced
- 1 ½ cups chicken stock
- ⅓ cup dry white wine
- 6 sprigs thyme
- 2 – 3 tbsp. arrowroot starch
- 2 – 3 tbsp. water
- 1 tbsp. butter (optional)

Preparation

1. Season the turkey breast all over with salt and black pepper.

2. Place the trivet into the Instant Pot. Add the vegetables, chicken stock and wine. Add the turkey breast skin-side up.

3. Place the lid on the Instant Pot and set to manual (more/high) for 25 minutes. When done allow the pressure to release naturally for 10 minutes. Do a quick release of the remaining pressure and remove the lid.

4. Remove the turkey breast to a pre-warmed serving dish and cover with aluminum foil. If you have a meat thermometer check the temperature is 165 ºF (74 ºC) in the thickest part of the breast. If not place it back in the pot and cook it for another few minutes on high.

5. Skim off any excess fat from the sauce and remove the thyme stalks. Remove the trivet.

6. Set the instant pot to Sauté (normal).

7. Dissolve the arrowroot starch in water. Gradually whisk in the arrowroot starch until you have the desired thickness. Whisk in the butter. It's optional but it does enrich the sauce. Taste the sauce and season with salt and pepper if desired.

8. Pour the sauce over the turkey breast.

Cooking tips

The skin will not crisp up when cooked in a pressure cooker. If you prefer crispy skin remove the breast to a baking tray and place under a pre-heated broiler until browned and crispy. You can substitute arrowroot starch with cornstarch but it is not gluten free.

Turkey legs with portobello mushrooms

||||||||||||||||||||||||||||||||||||||||||||||||||||||||||||||||||||||||||||||||||||||||||||||||||||||||||||||

This simple recipe makes a nice change from turkey breasts. The sherry wine, sherry vinegar and Portobello mushrooms add wonderful depth of flavour and earthiness to the dish. Serve with creamy mashed potatoes spiked with finely grated Parmesan cheese and parsley.

Details

Preparation Time: 10 minutes

Cooking Time: 30 minutes

Serves: 4

Kcal per serve: 880

Ingredients

- 2 turkey legs
- Sea salt and black pepper to taste
- 2 tbsp. olive oil
- 2 rashers smoked bacon, chopped
- 1 medium red onion, diced
- 1 large carrot, peeled and diced
- 1 stalk celery, diced
- 1 cup Portobello mushrooms, diced
- 4 cloves garlic, minced
- 2 tbsp. sweet sherry wine
- 1 tsp. sherry vinegar
- 2 tsp. Worcestershire/soy sauce
- 1 cup chicken stock
- ½ tsp. dried rosemary
- ½ tsp. dried thyme
- 2 bay leaves

Preparation

1. Season the turkey legs with salt and pepper to taste.

2. Set the instant pot to Sauté (more/high) and add the oil. When hot sauté the chicken legs until browned all over. Remove and set aside in a bowl.

3. Set to Sauté (normal) and add the bacon, onions, carrot, celery and mushrooms and sauté for 4 – 5 minutes until the onions are soft. Add the garlic and sauté for another minute.

4. Add the sherry and vinegar and cook for a minute before adding the stock and Worcestershire sauce. Stir to scrap off any browned bits from the bottom of the pan.

5. Add the herbs and season with salt and pepper to taste. Add the turkey legs and any resting juice. Set to manual (more/high) for 18 minutes. When done allow the pressure to decrease naturally for 10 minutes before releasing the remaining pressure manually.

6. Adjust the seasoning with salt and pepper to taste if desired.

Cooking tips

If you want a thicker sauce remove the turkey legs to a warmed serving dish. Dissolve 2 – 3 tablespoons of cornstarch in water. Set to Sauté (Normal) and slowly add the cornstarch, stirring constantly, until you have the desired thickness. Pour the sauce over the turkey legs.

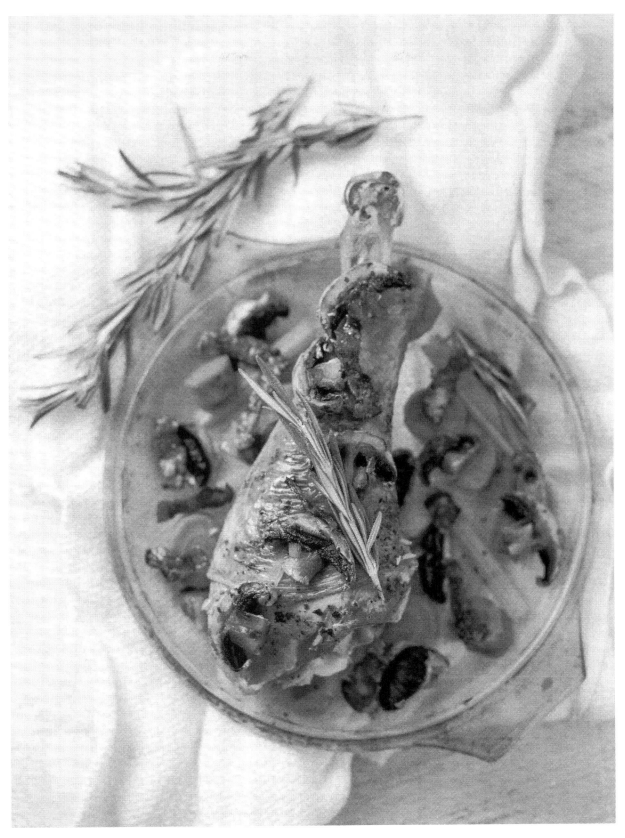

Turkey wings with cranberries & pecan nuts

||||||||||||||||||||||||||||||||||||||||||||||||||||||||||||||||||||||||||||||||||||||||||||||||||||

Turkey wings are an often unforgotten and un-liked part of the turkey as they can be a bit dry when roasted. But pressure-cooked they remain tender and juicy and have a similar quantity of meat as a medium-sized chicken leg. Use can also swop pecans for nuts of choice such as walnut, macadamia, pistachio, almond or cashew nuts.

Details

Preparation Time: 10 minutes

Cooking Time: 25 minutes

Serves: 4

Kcal per serve: 890

Ingredients

- 4 turkey wings
- salt and black pepper to taste
- 1 tbsp. canola or olive oil
- 1 tbsp. unsalted butter
- 1 medium onion, diced
- 1 stalk celery, diced
- ½ cup fresh orange juice
- zest of ½ orange
- ½ cup chicken or turkey stock
- 1 cup Craisins (dried cranberries), cover with boiling water and soak for 5 mins.
- 1 cup pecan nuts, roughly chopped
- 10 stalks thyme
- 1 tsp. thyme leaves for garnish.

Preparation

1. Season the turkey wings with salt and pepper to taste.

2. Set the instant pot to Sauté (more/high) and add the oil and butter. When hot brown the wings on all sides. Remove and set aside.

3. Set the instant pot to Sauté (less/low) and add the onion, celery and garlic. Sauté for 2 minutes until the onions are soft. Add the orange juice and stock and deglaze the pot. Add the remaining ingredients and stir to combine. Add the wings back to the pot and push down under the liquid and ingredients.

4. Secure the lid and set the instant pot to manual (more/high) for 15 minutes (20 for large wings). When done allow the pressure to release naturally for 10 minutes. Do a quick release of the remaining pressure and remove the lid.

5. Discard the thyme stalks.

6. Remove the turkey breast to a pre-warmed serving dish and cover with aluminum foil.

7. Set the instant pot to Sauté (more/high) and reduce the sauce by half. Taste and adjust the seasoning with salt and pepper if desired.

8. Pour the sauce over the turkey wings and scatter over the fresh thyme leaves.

Cooking tips

The skin will not crisp up when cooked in a pressure cooker. If you prefer crispy skin remove the wings to a baking tray and place under a pre-heated broiler until crispy and browned.

Turkey meatballs with blueberries and balsamic

||||||||||||||||||||||||||||||||||||||||||||||||||||||||||||||||||||||||||||||||||||||||||||||||||||||||||||||||||||||||||||||||||||

This versatile dish is great served as a main course with fresh egg pasta such as tagliatelle or as an appetizer for 8 people. Quick and easy to prepare, these deliciously fruity meatballs and will be a party favourite. Fresh is best but frozen blueberries can be used.

Details

Preparation Time: 15 minutes

Cooking Time: 10 minutes

Serves: 2

Kcal per serve: 670

Ingredients

- 1 lb. ground turkey
- 1 small onion, finely chopped
- 2 cloves garlic, minced
- 2 tsp. Worcestershire/soy sauce
- 3 tbsp. panko bread crumbs
- 1 egg, beaten
- ¼ tsp. freshly ground black pepper, or to taste
- 3 tbsp. parmesan cheese, finely grated
- 1 tsp. Italian herb seasoning

Blueberry sauce
- 8 oz. (1 ½ cups) blueberries (plus 2 tbsp. for garnish)
- ⅓ cup granulated white sugar
- ½ tsp kosher sea salt, or to taste
- ½ tsp. black pepper, or to taste
- 2 sprigs fresh rosemary
- 2 sprig fresh thyme
- 1 ½ tsp. balsamic vinegar

Preparation

1. Add all the blueberry sauce ingredients to the Instant Pot. Stir to combine and set to Manual (more/high) for 5 minutes. When done do a quick release of the pressure and remove the lid.

2. Add all the meatball ingredients to a large bowl and mix together. Form the mixture into 1" meatballs.

3. Add the meatballs to the pot ensuring they are covered by the sauce. Set to Manual (More/High) for 5 minutes. When done do a quick release of the pressure.

4. Serve garnished with a scattering of blueberries.

Cooking tips

Reduce the calories by 258kcal and make it more diabetic- friendly by substituting granulated white sugar with stevia. It has zero calories and does not raise blood sugar levels. Convert as per the brand of stevia and type (granulated, powdered, liquid etc.) you are using e.g. 4 tsp. Truvia Spoonable for ⅓ cup sugar.

Turkey & bean chili

||||||||||||||||||||||||||||||||||||||||||||||||||||||||||||||||||||||||||||||||||||||||||||||||||||||||||||

This is an easy to prepare chili that tastes even better the following day! Lean turkey breast and protein packed kidney beans make this a healthy, low-fat and economical dish that is full of spicy flavours. Add a little indulgence to the chili and serve with a dollop of crème fraiche or sour cream.

Details

Preparation Time: 10 minutes (plus 12 hours for soaking beans)

Cooking Time: 30 minutes

Serves: 3

Kcal per serve: 670

Ingredients

- 2 cups (approx. 14oz.) red kidney beans
- 2 tbsp. olive oil
- 1 ½ lb. turkey breast, diced into 1" cubes
- 1 red onion, diced
- 1 medium green bell pepper, diced
- 1 medium red bell pepper, diced
- 1 stalk celery, finely sliced
- 4 cloves garlic, minced
- 1 tsp. cumin seeds
- 2 cups chicken or veal stock
- 1 can (14.5 oz.) chopped tomatoes
- 2 tbsp. tomato paste
- ½ tsp. red pepper flakes, or to taste
- ½ tsp. cayenne pepper, or to taste
- 1 tsp. sweet smoked paprika
- ½ tsp. black pepper
- 1 tsp. dried thyme
- ½ tsp. dried oregano
- 2 bay leaves
- 1 small bunch cilantro, chopped
- cilantro leaves for garnish

Preparation

1. Soak the beans in a large bowl of water for 12 hours or overnight.

2. Season the turkey pieces with salt and black pepper to taste. Set the Instant Pot to Sauté (more/high) and add the oil. When the oil is hot sauté the turkey pieces, in batches, until nicely browned. Set aside in a bowl.

3. Set to Sauté (normal) and add the onion, bell peppers, celery, garlic and cumin seeds. Sauté for 4 minutes until the onions are soft.

4. Add the turkey pieces and resting juices, stock, tomatoes, tomato paste, spices and dried herbs and stir to combine. Set to manual (more/high) for 25 minutes. Allow to release pressure naturally for 10 minutes before releasing the remaining pressure. Remove the lid.

5. Set to Sauté (normal) and simmer for 3 - 5 minutes, stirring constantly, to reduce and thicken the sauce. Add the cilantro for the last minute of simmering.

6. Serve garnished with a sprinkle of cilantro leaves and (optional) a dollop of sour cream or crème fraiche.

Cooking tips

You can save the soaking time for the beans by pre- cooking them. Add 8 cups of water and a teaspoon of salt to the Instant Pot. Rinse the beans and add to the pot. Set to manual (more/high) for 2 minutes. Slowly release the pressure. Strain the beans and rinse under cold water.

Red coconut curry turkey

|||||||||||||||||||||||||||||||||||||||||||||||||||||||||||||||||||||||||||||||||||||||||||||||||||||||||||||||||||||||||||||||||||||||||||||||||||||||||

Give your turkey dinner a completely interesting twist of Thai. Creamy, spicy, tangy... this Asian red curry dish delivers an explosion of flavors with every bite.

Details

Preparation Time: 15 minutes

Cooking Time: 25 minutes

Serves: 3

Kcal per serve: 670

Ingredients

- 1lb (450gr) Turkey Breast Fillet, cut into 2" pieces
- 2 Large Tomatoes, quartered
- 1 Eggplant, cut into inch pieces
- 2 tablespoons Coconut Oil
- 1 tablespoon Minced Garlic
- 1 tablespoon Minced Ginger
- 1 tablespoon Minced Shallots
- 2 tablespoons Red Curry Paste
- 1 cup Coconut Cream
- ½ cup Chicken Stock
- 1 tablespoon Fish Sauce
- Lime Wedges
- Fresh Cilantro

Preparation

1. Set pot to sauté mode.

2. Heat coconut oil.

3. Add garlic, ginger, and shallots. Sauté briefly.

4. Add red curry paste and sauté until aromatic. About 2 minutes.

5. Pour coconut cream and stock into the pot. Bring to a simmer.

6. Add turkey cook on high pressure for 15 minutes. Release pressure.

7. Switch pot to sauté mode, then add tomatoes and eggplants. Cover and simmer for 5-7 minutes.

8. Serve with lime wedges on the side.

Cooking tips

Make this curry a more complete meal by adding fresh vegetables of your choice. Chopped green beans, winter bamboo shoots, and a variety of mushrooms would all be ideal. Also, feel free to use more chili for a more authentic local Thai dining experience!

Turkey with avocado relish

Healthy fats and protein are your secret weapon for weight loss. This quick cooking healthy dinner combines the leanness of turkey with the savory goodness of spices to make an amazing dinner.

Details

Prep Time: 5 minutes

Cooking Time: 10 minutes

Serves: 2

Kcal per serve: 745

Ingredients

- 225g turkey cutlets
- ½ tsp 5-spice powder
- 2 tbsp. extra virgin olive oil
- 1 tbsp. chili powder
- A good pinch kosher salt

For the avocado relish:

- ½ avocado, diced
- 1 seedless orange, cut into segments • and discarding the membranes
- 1 small Vidalia onion, minced
- 1 tsp. apple cider vinegar
- 1 tbsp. fresh cilantro, chopped

Preparation

1. Combine the avocado, orange segments, onion, vinegar and cilantro and toss well to combine.

2. Next, combine all the spices for the turkey in a shallow bowl then dredge the cutlets in the spice mix.

3. Add the oil to your instant pot set on sauté mode and sear the turkey until cooked to desired doneness for about 3-5 minutes on each side.

4.Add a cup of water and cook on manual for 5 minutes and then let pressure come down on its own.

5.Serve hot with the relish. Enjoy!

Braised turkey breast, shiitake and tofu

|||||||||||||||||||||||||||||||||||||||||||||||||||||||||||||||||||||||||||||||||||||||||||||||||||||||||||||||||||||

The inclusion of tofu and shiitake mushrooms together with braised turkey, makes of this dish a leaner alternative to the traditional Shandong or Taiwanese recipe for braised pork belly and steamed rice. Turkey has fewer calories, which makes this recipe wonderful for those watching their calories but still loving braised meat dishes.

Details

Prep Time: 20 minutes

Cooking Time: 15 minutes

Serves: 2

Kcal per serve: 670

Ingredients

- 400 grams of boneless turkey breast (14.0 oz)
- 100 grams of firm white tofu (3.5 oz)
- 4 dried shiitake mushrooms
- 2 fresh Cayenne peppers into 1-cm strips
- 1 cup of diced onions,
- 2 tbsp. chopped shallots
- 2 tbsp. chopped garlic
- 2 medium tomatoes
- ¼ cup of dark soy sauce
- 4 tbsp. light soy sauce

Spices
- 4 star anises
- 1 cinnamon stick
- 5 cloves
- 1 bay leaf
- 1 slice of ginger root, 0.5-inch thick
- 2 tbsps. coconut oil
- 2.5 cups of water or chicken stock
- Salt and pepper to taste
- 2 hardboiled eggs

Preparation

1. Soak the dried shiitake mushrooms in warm water. Once they are hydrated, remove the stalks and cut each mushroom to 4-5 smaller pieces. To save time, put the mushrooms in a bowl of water and leave it in the fridge overnight. The next day, the mushrooms are already well-hydrated and easy to cut.

2. Cut the white firm tofu to 1-inch cubes. Pan sear the tofu on all sides on a non-stick frying pan for 30 seconds on each side or until you can see streaks of golden brown on the tofu skin. The tofu needs this searing to maintain their firm texture during cooking.

3. Cut the turkey into about 1-inch bite-sized pieces or slightly larger.

4. Cut 8x8-cm piece out of a cheesecloth. Place the star anise, ginger, cinnamon stick, cloves, and bay leaf on the cloth. Wrap and tie with a string to make a bundle. Do not use plastic string or plastic ribbon as we are going to boil the spices in the broth along with the turkey.

5. Heat the coconut oil in the Instant Pot.

6. Add the diced onions, shallots, cayenne pepper, and garlic. Stir until fragrant and you can see the onions have turned translucent. Don't let the garlic or shallots burn as it gives a bitter taster.

7. Add the chopped turkey breast and stir fry until the turkey meat starts to change color.

8. Add the mushrooms. Stir fry for 2-3 minutes. Add the chicken stock or water, dark sweet soy sauce and light sweet soy sauce, and diced tomato.

9. Add the tofu and the spices that are wrapped in the bag of cheesecloth.

10. Lock the lid and cook on high pressure for 15 minutes.

11. Let the pressure release naturally.

12. Take the spices wrapped in cheesecloth out of the pot.

13. Continue to simmer to allow some of the braising juice to evaporate.

14. Add the hardboiled eggs.

15. Adjust seasoning with salt and pepper.

16. Serve on top of a bowl of steamed rice.

Moroccan lemon, lime and olive turkey thighs

|||||||||||||||||||||||||||||||||||||||||||||||||||||||||||||||||||||||||||||||||||||||||||||||||||||||||||||||||||||||||||||||||||||||

An explosion of aromatic and spicy flavours from North Africa: saffron, cumin and cinnamon. Make it even spicier by replacing the sweet paprika with the hot smoked variety. Add chickpeas for additional texture. Herb- or lemon-flavored couscous combined with dried chopped apricots and parsley will complete the dish.

Details

Prep Time: 15 minutes

Cooking Time: 30 minutes

Serves: 4

Kcal per serve: 1150

Ingredients

- 4 x1⅓ lb. turkey thighs, skinless and boneless
- 1 tbsp. olive oil
- 12 green olives, pitted
- ½ cup almond or cashew nuts
- ½ lemon, 1 lime, quartered
- 2 cloves garlic, crushed
- 1 tbsp. sun-dried tomatoes in oil, into strips
- 1 medium red onion, diced
- ¼ cup seedless raisins or chopped dates
- 2 cups chicken or turkey stock
- ½ tsp. ground cinnamon
- ¼ tsp. saffron powder
- ½ tsp. smoked sweet paprika
- ¼ tsp. black pepper
- ½ tsp. chili powder
- 1 cup fresh cilantro, chopped
- ½ tsp. ground cumin
- Salt to taste

Preparation

1. Add all the ingredients except for the turkey and half of the cilantro into the Instant Pot. Stir well to combine.

2. Add the turkey thighs and stir well to combine, ensuring that you press them below the surface of the ingredients.

3. Lock the lid and cook on high pressure for 30 minutes.

4. Release the pressure and add the reserved cilantro.

5. Transfer to a serving dish and garnish with cilantro leaves.

6. Optional: If desired, you can thicken the sauce with 1 or 2 spoonfuls of cornstarch or arrowroot into little cold water. Add the hot sauce, stirring constantly until the sauce thickens to the desired consistency.

Cooking tips

Can also be made with a turkey leg, or a combination of a thigh and a leg, either boneless or bone-in. The skin can be left on, but that will make the dish a little fattier. If you can't get turkey, use a bone-in, skinless whole chicken leg or else a thigh-drumstick combination.

Instant pot stuffed turkey breast roast

|||||||||||||||||||||||||||||||||||||||||||||||||||||||||||||||||||||||||||||||||||||||||||||||||||||||||

Give your family a mini Christmas feast with a combination of turkey breast stuffed and loaded with turkey mince. The mince is cooked with eggs and powdered spices to add some spice and flavour, while the eggs serve as a protein source to your diet.

Details

Prep Time: 15 minutes

Cooking Time: 25 minutes

Serves: 4

Kcal per serve: 690

Ingredients

- 2 tbsp fresh ginger-garlic paste
- 2 tsp red chili flakes
- ½ cup Greek Yogurt
- Salt and black pepper, as per taste
- 2 tablespoons extra virgin olive oil
- 4 turkey breasts
- 4 onions, minced or grated
- 5-6 garlic cloves, peeled and minced
- 1 teaspoon carom seeds
- 2 tomatoes, finely chopped
- 2 teaspoons red chili powder
- ½ teaspoon turmeric powder
- 3 eggs
- Juice of half lemon
- 200 grams turkey mince (boneless) (7.1 oz)

Preparation

1. Take a mixing bowl and combine the yoghurt with the ginger-garlic paste, red chili flakes along with some salt and pepper.

2. Wash and pat dry the turkey breast and slit them into half from the center lengthwise. Pour some olive oil and the prepared marinade all over the breast and spread it well. Place the marinated turkey breast in the refrigerator and let it rest for around an hour or so.

3. Meanwhile, heat some olive oil in the Instant Pot. Add the mince onion and garlic along with the carom seeds. Fry for 3-4 minutes and then add the tomatoes. After a couple of minutes, add the lemon juice, red chili powder, turmeric and eggs. Stir it in vigorously to scramble the eggs well. Add in turkey mince and mix well.

4. Thereafter place the turkey breast and pour in some water (around a cup or so, as needed). Lock the lid and cook on high pressure for 25 minutes.

5. Release pressure naturally.

Cooking tips

Mix some balsamic vinegar to the turkey mince for more added flavour. Add a shot of bourbon towards the end or just before serving the turkey.

Instant pot turkey with sage and thyme rubs

||||||||||||||||||||||||||||||||||||||||||||||||||||||||||||||||||||||||||||||||||||||||||||||||||||||||||||||||||||||||||||

A no-hassle variation of the baked version makes a wonderful choice for those new at cooking turkey dishes. Feeding dinner guests has never been so easy! To ensure this typically bland-tasting meat tastes wonderful, use a six-pound turkey to begin with and then larger sizes as you become more used to preparing the recipe.

Details

Prep Time: 15-20 minutes

Cooking Time: 30 minutes

Serves: 4

Kcal per serve: 925

Ingredients

- 6lb. whole turkey
- 1/4 cup of salt
- 1/4 cup of ground pepper
- 2 tbsps ground cumin
- 2 tbsps dried thyme
- 2 tablespoons dried rosemary
- 1 teaspoon allspice
- 1 tsp chicken bouillon granules
- ½ tbsp cayenne pepper powder
- 1 tbsp brown sugar
- 3 tbsp coconut oil
- 2 cups of chicken broth

Preparation

1. Prepare the turkey rub. In a bowl, with a spoon, mix the salt, ground black pepper, ground cumin, dried thyme, dried rosemary, all-spice powder, cayenne pepper (if using), brown sugar, and coconut oil. Stir well until everything is combined. Set aside.

2. Pat the turkey dry with clean kitchen towel. Rub the outer part of the turkey and inside the skin with the dry mixture. Then, rub some of the seasonings in the turkey cavity.

3. Add two cups of water into the Instant Pot. Add turkey and cook on high pressure for 30 minutes.

4. Let the pressure release naturally.

5. Take the turkey out of the pot. Carve or cut according to your preferred serving size and serve in individual plates along with the side dishes.

Cooking tips

If you are not going to entertain many people, you may use chicken instead of turkey. Choose the best quality, organic and free range whole chicken that you can get. Try mixing different spices, typically rosemary, thyme, sage, oregano go well with lemon juice and olive oil, while onion powder, garlic powder, all-spice works well with lime and coconut oil.

Red coconut curry turkey

||||||||||||||||||||||||||||||||||||||||||||||||||||||||||||||||||||||||||||||||||||||||||||||||||||||||||||||||||||||||||||||||||||||

Give your turkey dinner a unique Thai twist: Creamy, spicy, tangy... this Asian red curry dish delivers an explosion of flavours with every bite.

Details

Preparation Time: 15 minutes

Cooking Time: 15 minutes

Serves: 4

Kcal per serve: 500

Ingredients

- 1lg. (450 gr) Turkey Breast Fillet, cut into 2" pieces
- 2 Large Tomatoes, quartered
- 1 Eggplant, cut into inch pieces
- 2 tablespoons Coconut Oil
- 1 tablespoon Minced Garlic
- 1 tablespoon Minced Ginger
- 1 tablespoon Minced Shallots
- 2 tablespoons Red Curry Paste
- 1 cup Coconut Cream
- ½ cup Chicken Stock
- 1 tablespoon Fish Sauce
- Lime Wedges
- Fresh Cilantro

Preparation

1. Set pot to sauté mode.

2. Heat coconut oil.

3. Add garlic, ginger, and shallots. Sauté briefly.

4. Add red curry paste and sauté until aromatic. About 2 minutes.

5. Pour coconut cream and stock into the pot. Bring to a simmer.

6. Add turkey cook on high pressure for 15 minutes. Release pressure.

7. Switch pot to sauté mode, then add tomatoes and eggplants. Cover and simmer for 5-7 minutes.

8. Serve with lime wedges on the side.

Cooking tips

Make this curry a more complete meal by adding fresh vegetables of your choice. Chopped green beans, winter bamboo shoots, and a variety of mushrooms would all be ideal. Also, feel free to use more chili for a more authentic local Thai dining experience!

Instant pot turkey mole poblano

||||||||||||||||||||||||||||||||||||||||||||||||||||||||||||||||||||||||||||||||||||||||||||||||||||||||||||||||||||

A unique Mexican cooking sauce mixing at perfection peanut butter, cocoa, cumin, cinnamon, red peppers, onions and garlic. Locally known as "the mole", this versatile sauce works well for a variety of meat and poultry dishes including this instant pot turkey mole poblano.

Details

Preparation Time: 5 minutes

Cooking Time: 20 minutes

Serves: 4

Kcal per serve: 670

Ingredients

- 1lb. (450g) Turkey Breast Fillets

For the Marinade
- ½ tsp. Salt
- ½ tsp. Pepper
- ½ tsp. Garlic Powder
- ½ tsp. Cinnamon Powder
- ½ tsp. Cumin Powder
- ¼ tsp. Red Pepper Flakes
- 1 tbsp. Lime Juice

For the Mole Sauce
- 1 Large Roma Tomato, chopped
- ½ White Onion, chopped
- 1 clove Garlic, mashed
- 1 Serrano Pepper, sliced
- 1 tbsp. Sesame Seeds, toasted
- 2 cups Chicken Broth
- Salt and Pepper
- 2 tbsp. Canola Oil
- 1 cup Creamy Peanut Butter
- ¼ cup Cocoa Powder

Preparation

1. Combine all ingredients for the marinade in a bowl. Rub over the turkey breasts and leave to marinate overnight.

2. Combine all ingredients for the mole paste in a blender. Process into a smooth paste.

3. Arrange turkey breasts inside the pot.

4. Pour mole sauce together with half a cup of chicken stock and cook on high pressure for 15 minutes. Release pressure.

Cooking tips

Any type of poultry would go excellently with a mole sauce. In fact, other meats such as pork or beef would come out equally well. Like your mole a bit on the spicier side? Chop up more of those serranos!

Juniper and citrus turkey leg confit

||||||||||||||||||||||||||||||||||||||||||||||||||||||||||||||||||||||||||||||||||||||||||||||||||||||||||||||||

Super flavourful red turkey leg meat, with a fresh aromatic blend of juniper berries and citrus essence, poached slowly until fall-off-the-bone tender, then finished crisp under the broiler. Simply exquisite.

Details

Preparation Time: 30 minutes

Cooking Time: 4 hours

Serves: 4

Kcal per serve: 600

Ingredients

- 2 Turkey Drumsticks
- 8 Juniper Berries, rough-chopped
- Zest of 1 Orange
- Zest of 2 Lemons
- 1 tablespoon Black Peppercorns, crushed
- 2 teaspoons Coarse Salt
- 2 cups Olive Oil

Preparation

1. Combine all ingredients in a bowl and leave to marinate overnight.

2. Transfer turkey drumsticks and marinade into the pot.

3. Set pot to slow cooker mode on low and leave for 4 hours. Leave to release pressure naturally.

4. Carefully take the turkey legs out of the pot and transfer to a baking sheet.

5. Roast in the oven for 15-20 minutes at 220C.

Cooking tips

Getting the turkey legs completely submerged in olive oil is key to making this confit. Preparing this dish in large batches (more turkey legs), would considerably save you from using much more oil. Feel free to add some sprigs of fresh herb into the pot for more aroma. Tarragon and rosemary would be excellent choices.

Vegetarian Recipes

||||||||||||||||||||||||||||||||||||||||||||||||||

Instant pot zucchini shakshuka

A Middle Eastern breakfast dish that will surely get you get you up and going for the rest of your day. The goodness of zucchini, tomatoes, peppers, and onions come together to elevate a simple egg dish, which is further spiced with garlic, paprika, and cumin. If you thought that bacon was ideal companion for eggs, think again.

Details

Preparation Time: 10 minutes

Cooking Time: 10 minutes

Serves: 1

Kcal per serve: 885

Ingredients

- 1 large Zucchini, spiralized or cut into thin strips 1 White Onion, diced
- 1 large Red Bell Pepper, diced
- 4 cloves Garlic, finely minced
- ½ tsp. Paprika
- ½ tsp. Cumin Powder
- 14 oz can Diced Tomatoes ¼ cup Vegetable Stock
- 4 Eggs
- 1 tbsp. Olive Oil
- Salt, to taste
- Pepper, to taste

Preparation

1. Set pot to sauté mode.

2. Heat olive oil.

3. Sauté onions, garlic, and bell pepper until onions are translucent.

4. Add zucchini and sauté for another minute.

5. Add diced tomatoes, paprika, cumin, and vegetable stock. Simmer for 3-5 minutes.

6. Season with salt and pepper.

7. Make a dent over the vegetables for each of the eggs.

8. Crack a whole egg into each dent.

9. Switch pot to keep warm setting and leave for 3-5 minutes or until eggs come to desired doneness.

Cooking tips

Don't be limited by the exclusive use of zucchini for this healthier version of shakshuka. Consider thin slices of carrots, squash, or asparagus as well.

Korean eggplant and rice cake stew

A vegetable and rice cake stew inspired by the spicy classic Korean soup Tteokbokki. An excellent mix of spices in an umami-rich broth, this is truly a dish worth trying

Details

Preparation Time: 5 minutes

Cooking Time: 35 minutes

Serves: 2

Kcal per serve: 770

Ingredients

- 450 gr (1lb.) Eggplants, split in half lengthwise and cut into 2" batons
- 225 grams (1/2 lb.) Sticky Rice Cakes, cut into 2" lengths
- 1 Onion, diced
- 4 stalks Leeks, cut into inch pieces
- 1 liter Vegetable Stock
- 1 tsp Dashi or Vegetable broth Powder
- ¼ cup Gochujang(Korean Hot Pepper Paste)
- 2 tablespoons Soy Sauce
- pinch of Sugar

Preparation

1. Soak the rice cakes in cold water for at least 30 minutes.

2. Combine all ingredients inside the pot and cook for 4 minutes on high pressure. Release pressure.

3. Adjust seasoning with soy sauce and sugar if needed.

Cooking tips

If available, use some dried kelp for the stock for more depth of flavor. More Gochujang may also be used for additional heat. Adding slices of fish cake, vegetarian concerns aside, would also be highly recommended.

Instant pot baked Provençale tomatoes

|||||||||||||||||||||||||||||||||||||||||||||||||||||||||||||||||||||||||||||||||||||||||||||||||||||||||||||||||||||||||||||||||||

Plump, juicy, perfectly ripe tomatoes baked in an aromatic blend of the popular Herbes de Provence. Excellent on its own, paired with a dish of grilled meat or fish, putting on top of some crisp crostini, or tossed with freshly cooked pasta, this dish will make and of your guest´s day with their very first bit.

Details

Preparation Time: 10 minutes

Cooking Time: 4h

Serves: 1

Kcal per serve: 850

Ingredients

- 8 large Tomatoes, cut into halves
- 1 teaspoon Chopped Marjoram
- 1 teaspoon Chopped Rosemary
- 1 teaspoon Chopped Thyme
- 4 cloves Garlic, minced
- 1/2 cup Extra-Virgin Olive Oil
- Salt
- Freshly Ground Black Pepper
- Optional, ½ cup Grated Parmesan Cheese

Preparation

1. Combine tomatoes, chopped herbs, minced garlic, olive oil, black pepper, and salt inside the pot.

2. Leave to cook on slow cooker mode set to low for 4 hours.

3. Transfer to a serving bowl and top with grated parmesan.

Cooking tips

Other herbs from the Provençale region such as oregano, tarragon, and parsley may also be substituted or added altogether... you couldn't go wrong.

Tasty spiced pecans

For a nutty, savoury and delicious dessert treat, our low carb candied pecans take the crown! It's not only healthy but also very satisfying.

Details

Preparation Time: 10 minutes

Cooking Time: 15 minutes

Serves: 8

Kcal per serve: 410

Ingredients

- 4 cups raw pecans
- 1/8 tsp. cayenne pepper
- 1/8 tsp. ground ginger
- 1/2 tsp. ground nutmeg
- 1 tsp. ground cinnamon
- 1/8 tsp. sea salt
- 1 tbsp. water

Preparation

1.Combine all ingredients in your instant pot and lock lid; cook on manual for 10 minutes and then quick release the pressure.

2. Transfer the mixture to a baking sheet and spread it out; bake at 350 degrees for about 5 minutes.

Cooking tips

Chop the pecans into halves to create a more surface area for a larger spice coating to nut ratio. Add these pecans add a salad for an extra bit of crunchiness.

Linguini with mixed mushroom ragout

High in antioxidants and low in calorie: it is well known mushrooms are wonderfully healthy... and this simple dish only proves that not only they are good for your health but also incredibly tasty! Too good to be true?

Details

Preparation Time: 15 minutes

Cooking Time: 4h

Serves: 2

Kcal per serve: 700

Ingredients

- 1lb.(450gr) Mushrooms cleaned and sliced
- 1 White Onion chopped
- 6 Garlic cloves minced
- 1 teaspoon Ground Black Pepper
- 1.5 cups Vegetable Stock
- ½ cup Red Wine
- 1 can Diced Tomatoes
- 2 tablespoons Chopped Basil
- 2 tablespoons Olive Oil
- ½ lb. (225 gr) Linguini, cooked to package directions
- Salt, to taste

Preparation

1. Set pot to slow cooker mode on low.

2. Combine mushrooms, onions, pepper, vegetable stock, red wine, tomatoes, basil, and diced tomatoes inside the pot.

3. Cook for 4 hours.

4. Season with salt to taste.

5. Ladle over hot linguini.

6. Top with a drizzle of olive oil before serving.

Cooking tips

Make this ragout even healthier by using your favorite gluten-free pasta. Top with some shaved parmesan or chopped fresh herbs to elevate the flavors even further. For some heat, a pinch of red pepper flakes would be great!

Coconut and chili green beans

||||||||||||||||||||||||||||||||||||||||||||||||||||||||||||||||||||||||||||||||||||||||||||||||||||||||||||||

A quick and easy Asian vegetable stir-fry conveniently adapted for your Instant Pot. Creamy and perfectly spicy, this all-in-one dish will surely awaken everyone's taste buds!

Details

Preparation Time: 5 minutes

Cooking Time: 10 minutes

Serves: 2

Kcal per serve: 600

Ingredients

- 1lb.(450gr) Green Beans, cut into ½" pieces
- 1/2 lb. (225 gr)Sliced Tofu
- 1.5 cups Coconut Milk
- 4 Garlic, cloves minced
- 1 Shallot, thinly sliced
- 2-3 Pieces Red Thai Chili, chopped
- 1 tablespoon Fish Sauce

Preparation

1. Set pot to sauté mode.

2. Heat coconut oil.

3. Add ground pork and sauté until slightly brown.

4. Put the shallots, the garlic and of course the chili. Sauté well until aromatic.

5. Add green beans and sauté until a bit tender.

6. Add coconut milk and fish sauce. Simmer for 5 minutes.

Cooking tips

To suit a strict vegetarian diet, pan-fried tofu may be substituted for the ground pork. Vegan varieties of fish sauce can also be easily had from most specialty health shops.

Cauliflower and chickpea curry

Nothing beats the fresh and intense flavours after preparing your own curry paste from scratch. This combined with the richness of coconut cream, freshness of basil leaves, and the aromatic heat of Thai chilis make a complex-flavoured dish. A cauliflower and chickpeas curry that will certainly be welcomed and loved by vegetarians and meat-lovers alike.

Details

Preparation Time: 10 minutes

Cooking Time: 10 minutes

Serves: 4

Kcal per serve: 550

Ingredients

- 1lb.(450gr) Cauliflower, cut into florets
- 1 can Chickpeas, drained and washed
- 1 Shallot, thinly sliced
- 1 x 400-ml (12oz) can Coconut Cream
- a handful Fresh Basil Leaves
- 2-4 Red Thai Chilis, chopped
- 1-2 tsp. Fish Sauce
- 1 tbsp. Olive Oil

For the Curry Paste
- 1 bunch fresh cilantro, roughly chopped
- 2 stalks lemongrass, tough part removed, rough-chopped
- 4 pieces green jalapeno peppers, roughly chopped
- 2 pieces shallots, peeled and roughly chopped
- 6 cloves garlic, peeled and roughly chopped
- 1 piece(about 4-inch long) Turmeric, peeled and roughly chopped
- 1 pc. Lime, juiced

Preparation

1. Combine all ingredients for the curry paste in a food processor. Pulse into a smooth paste.

2. Set pot to sauté mode.

3. Heat olive oil and roast the curry paste until aromatic. About 3-5 minutes.

4. Add the coconut cream into the pot and bring to a boil.

5. Add the cauliflower, chickpeas, shallots, and Thai chilli.

6. Switch to manual mode and cook on high pressure for 4 minutes. Release pressure.

7. Season with fish sauce and garnish with fresh Thai Basil.

Cooking tips

Turn this recipe into a heartier all-in-one-pot meal by adding more components such as meat, seafood, pan-fried tofu, eggplant slices, or wedged tomatoes.

Apple cranberry sauce with orange zest

||||||||||||||||||||||||||||||||||||||||||||||||||||||||||||||||||||||||||||||||||||||||||||||||||||||||||||||||||||||||

A wonderful side dish for both vegan and non-vegan meals. It works perfectly with meatloaf, Beef Wellington, roasted turkey, sautéd vegetables, grilled vegan cheese, or even quinoa balls. The sauce can be dropped over biscuits or toast for a fast breakfast. The sweetness of this dish arises from apple juice and fruit, making the use of refined sugar, superfluous.

Details

Preparation Time: 20 min.
Cooking Time: 30 minutes
Serves: 1
Kcal per serve: 770

Ingredients

- 17.5 z (500 gr) apples
- 2 cups of fresh cranberries or 1 cup if using dried cranberries
- 1 tbsp. orange zest
- 2 cups of pure organic apple juice
- 2 tbsp. of lemon juice
- 2 tsps. of pumpkin pie spice
- ¼ tsp. of salt

Preparation

1. Peel and cut out the cores of the apples. Remove the seeds. Chop the apples into 1-inch thickness.

2. Rinse your cranberries in cold water, drain.

3. Zest the orange to get 1 tablespoon of zest. If you prefer the sauce to have a stronger hint of orange, you may add 2 tablespoons of zest or a slice of dried tangerine peel, available in most Asian stores.

4. Juice half a lemon to get two tablespoons of juice.

5. Add the chopped apples, cranberries, orange zest, lemon juice, and organic apple juice to the Instant Pot. Add two teaspoons of pumpkin pie spice and ¼ teaspoon of salt.

6. Cook on high pressure for 30 minutes.

7. Release the pressure naturally.

8. For a softer texture, you may mash the sauce using a potato masher at the end.

Cooking tips

Replace the pumpkin pie spice mix with small three-centimeter cinnamon sticks (the size of your little finger), two cloves, a pinch nutmeg (ground) and one to two-star anises. Remove them before using the potato masher.

Corn, pinto and quinoa enchilada with vegan cheese

||||||||||||||||||||||||||||||||||||||||||||||||||||||||||||||||||||||||||||||||||||||||||||||||||||||||||||||||||||||||||||||

Using vegan cheese, this enchilada is not only easy, but a crowd favourite. It will work equally well for non-vegetarian gourmets. Just spend time early in the day preparing the ingredients, put everything in the Instant Pot and wait.

Details

Preparation Time: 15-20 min.

Cooking time: 4 h and 30 minutes

Serves: 4

Kcal per serve: 750

Ingredients

- 1 cup of cooked pinto beans, drained
- ½ cup of dried tomatoes, drained and chopped
- 1 cup of corn, frozen or canned, drained
- 1 cup of quinoa, soaked in water first
- 1 cup of tomato sauce
- 2 cups of vegetable broth
- 2 tsps. cumin
- 1 tbsp. garlic, minced
- 1 tbsp. onion flakes
- 2 tbsps. all-purpose flour
- 2 cups of shredded vegan cheese (cheddar, mozzarella, or for-pasta)
- 1 tbsp. chili powder (optional)

Preparation

1. Rinse the quinoa in cold water. Then, soak in approximately half a cup of warm water while you prepare the rest of the ingredients.

2. Open the cans of your pinto beans, corn, and sun-dried tomatoes. Drain the sun-dried tomatoes and roughly chop into chunks. Peel and mince your garlic cloves (3-4) to get one tablespoon of minced garlic. Ground your cumin and measure to fill two teaspoons. Dilute the all-purpose flour in two tablespoons of water.

3. Set pot to slow cooker. Into the bowl, add quinoa, pinto beans, tomatoes, corn, tomato sauce, and chicken broth. Stir once or twice to combine. Then, add the ground cumin, minced garlic, onion flakes and chili powder (optional). Last, add the all-purpose flour that is diluted in water.

4. Set on High for 4 hours. After four hours, the quinoa should be soft. Add the shredded vegan cheese, sprinkling them on top. Cover again and cook for another 20-30 minutes or until the cheese melts. Serve in individual bowls with your preferred toppings (chopped parsley and avocado pieces are great toppings).

Cooking tips

These enchiladas are adaptable, you may substitute ingredients depending upon what you have on hand. You also can use different beans and grains. Great alternatives include black beans, fava beans, rice, lentils and chickpeas. For Dutch oven cooking: put ingredients in, cover, and bake for one and a half hours in a preheated. After 90 minutes, put in the cheese and bake for another twenty to thirty minutes, until the cheese has melted.

Instant pot red beans with fruity punch

||||||||||||||||||||||||||||||||||||||||||||||||||||||||||||||||||||||||||||||||||||||||||||||||||||||||||||||||||||||||||||||||||||||||

A light yet tasty Instant Pot variation of kidney beans infused with the kick of Balsamic vinegar and pineapples. Soak the beans overnight and put them into the Instant Pot with a combination of citrus fruits and sweet vegetables. Perfect for a lazy weekend afternoon.

Details

Prep Time: 15-20 minutes

Cooking Time: 10 minutes

Serves: 2

Kcal per serve: 650

Ingredients

- 9 oz (250gr) red kidney beans, soaked

- 2 tablespoons olive oil
- 1 large onion, chopped
- 1 tbsp fresh ginger-garlic paste
- 2 medium tomatoes, pureed
- 1 cup carrots, chopped
- 1 beetroot, chopped
- 2 slices pineapple, chopped
- 1 tablespoon Balsamic vinegar
- ½ sweet potato
- ½ cup cream
- Salt and black pepper,
- 2 teaspoons cumin powder

Preparation

1. Soak the beans overnight. Before cooking, drain them, preserving the water for cooking purposes.

2. Heat some oil in the instant pot and add the onions, along with the ginger-garlic paste.

3. As the onions are cooked, add the tomatoes, carrots and beetroot. Pour in some water which was used to soak the beans.

4. Add the beans, along with the chopped pineapples, sweet potato, Balsamic vinegar and some salt, cumin powder and some pepper.

5. Pour some more water and lock the lid. Cook on manual for 2 minutes. Release pressure naturally.

6. Mash the beans using s spatula and stir in the cream.

7. Simmer for 3-5 minutes.

8. Serve hot with steamed rice.

Cooking tips

Boil the beans separately, then cook them along with the vegetables. Choose adding lemon zest and lemon juice over the top for a zesty flavor. Also consider adding in black beans or chickpeas to increase the amount of protein.

Vegan mushroom lasagna

||||||||||||||||||||||||||||||||||||||||||||||||||||||||||||||||||||||||||||||||||||||||||||||||||||||||||||||||||||

A Lasagna requiring some preparation time on the stove for the sauce, but a hassle-free and swift assembly. Double it up and it still takes about the same amount of time to cook. Portobello mushrooms must be cooked on low heat and slowly, giving them time to mingle with the sweet basil and marinara sauce.

Details

Preparation time: 1h. 30 minutes

Serves: 4

Cooking time: 20 minutes

Kcal per serve: 500

Ingredients

- 7 oz (200 gr) fresh Portobello mushroom
- 1/2 cup of chopped sweet basil
- 1/2 cup onions, chopped
- 1 tbsp garlic, minced or pressed
- 3 medium-sized tomatoes, chopped
- 1 cup of canned crushed tomatoes
- 1/2 cup of red wine,
- 1 tsp Italian seasoning
- 1 tsp sea salt
- 1 tsp black pepper
- 1 tsp chili flakes
- 1/2 cup of vegetable broth
- 1 tbsp olive oil

Pasta
- 12 lasagna noodles
- 3 cups mozzarella

Béchamel
- 1 tbsp. olive oil
- ½ cup of onions
- ¼ cup of flour
- 2 cups of soy milk
- ½ tbsp. minced garlic
- salt and pepper

Preparation

1. Prepare the ingredients for the Marinara sauce. Chop the sweet basil, onions, and tomatoes. Remove the tomato seeds to make the sauce less sour(optional). Rinse the mushroom under cold tap water. Remove the gills and chop. Mince or press 3-4 cloves of garlic to fit 1 tablespoon.

2. Make the marinara sauce in a non-stick sauce pan. Heat the olive oil over medium heat. Add the onions and garlic until fragrant. After approximately 4-5 minutes, add the crushed and freshly chopped tomatoes, red wine, Italian seasoning, sea salt, black pepper, chili flakes. Stir to combine and cook the ingredients evenly for 3-4 minutes until the vegetables are soft. Add the sweet basil and Portobello mushroom pieces. Add half a cup of vegetable broth. Bring the sauce mixture to a boil. Turn off the heat when the sauce thickens and the vegetables are soft.

3. Prepare the ingredients for the bechamel sauce. Peel and chop the onions, mince your garlic. Measure the all-purpose flour to fill a quarter of a cup. Measure your soy milk. Mix the all-purpose flour with the soy milk in a small bowl. Stir thoroughly to make sure no lumps appear.

4. Make the bechamel sauce. In a non-stick sauce pan over medium heat, add the olive oil and sauté the onions and garlic until onions are translucent. Add the flour and soy milk mixture. Bring to a boil, stirring occasionally. Turn off the heat when the sauce thickens. Season the sauce with salt and pepper.

5. Assemble the lasagna. Layer the lasagna pasta, mushroom marinara, and bechamel alternately in a baking pan. Take one part of the marinara sauce and spread at the bottom. Then take one part of the Bechamel and spread over the marinara. Then, take 3-4 uncooked lasagna sheets and arrange them on top of the bechamel. Start from the second layer, top the bechamel sauce with a generous sprinkle of vegan mozzarella cheese. Repeat the process until you use up all the noodles and sauce.

6. Set the trivet inside the Instant Pot. Place the baking pan on top of the trivet. Close the lid and cook on manual for 20 minutes.

Vegetarian chickpea, quinoa and spinach chili

||||||||||||||||||||||||||||||||||||||||||||||||||||||||||||||||||||||||||||||||||||||||||||||||||||||||||||||||||||||||||||||||||

Chickpeas, quinoa, and spinach make a lovely trio ideal for a chili-based pot. Chickpeas are rich and creamy, the quinoa nutty and crunchy and finally the spinach brings a subtle bitterness that rounds everything up. Best of all, making it is extremely easy. All you must do is throwing all your ingredients into the Instant Pot, setting it and stirring every hour or so.

Details

Preparation Time: 10 min.

Cooking Time: 20 minutes

Serves: 1

Kcal per serve: 650

Ingredients

- 3 cups fresh spinach
- 1 ½ cups low salt vegetable broth,
- ½ cup uncooked quinoa
- 1 x15 oz. can diced tomatoes
- 1 x 15 oz. can chickpeas, drained
- 6 garlic cloves, minced
- 1 sweet red bell pepper, chopped
- 1 onion, diced
- 1 large carrot in 1-inch chunks
- 1 zucchini, chopped
- 2 tablespoons chili powder
- ½ tablespoon ground cumin
- Pinch of dried oregano
- 1 teaspoon soy sauce
- Juice of 1 lemon
- Kosher salt
- Black pepper

Preparation

1. Add all ingredients to the Instant Pot.

2. Stir to evenly distribute the spices.

3. Cover and cook on manual for 20 minutes.

4. Quick release the pressure.

5. Taste and adjust the seasoning as needed.

6. Ladle into bowls and serve.

Cooking tips

Feel free to adjust the amount of vegetable broth added to the chili for the desired consistency. Use the provided amount for a thick and hearty chili or add more if you prefer a loose one. Also, feel free to thinly slice a jalapeno or other spicy chili and add it in for more heat.

A 1000 Day Instant Pot Cooking Schedule

With the wide variety of recipes, cuisines, ingredients and tastes included in this book, feeling overwhelmed and not knowing what to cook and when is perfectly normal.

Luckily, to assist you when deciding what dishes to choose, we have created a 1000-day Instant Pot schedule, where all the recipes have been mixed and allocated to generate the maximum possible variety of dishes, so you never get stressed or bored.

In this schedule, you will find one Instant Pot recipe to be cooked every day. This does not mean you cannot do or should not do more than one, on the contrary!

But this has been done because not everyone has the time to cook more than once a day, and, for the sake of simplicity. The schedules are organized by months, where every month includes 4 weeks of seven days (Monday to Sunday).

Also, as indicated in the index of this part, there are some months that are specific to some people´s needs: Months 11 and 12 are dedicated to Vegetarian-Only recipes. On the other hand, month 29 includes recipes containing no pork.

I hope you enjoy this schedule very much and specially the recipes in it. I have put time and effort to make sure you have a great experience.

Katie Banks

Menu For Month 1

	Week 1	Week 2	Week 3	Week 4
Mon	Balsamic & Rosemary Roast Beef	Classic Beef Stew with Mushrooms and Peas	Hungarian Beef Goulash	South East Asian Beef Ribs and White Radish Stew
Tue	Marinara Beef Meatballs	Instant Pot Beef Crock Roast	Balsamic & Rosemary Roast Beef	Raised Beef Ribs
Wen	Spicy Citrus Beef	Instant Pot Marinara Beef Meatballs	Marinara Beef Meatballs	Instant Pot Beef Crock Roast
Thu	Hungarian Beef Goulash	Instant Pot Raised Beef Ribs	Raised Beef Ribs	Spicy Citrus Beef
Fri	Raised Beef Ribs	Balsamic & Rosemary Roast Beef	Instant Pot Beef Crock Roast	Marinara Beef Meatballs
Sat	Cherry Cheesecake	Pears Poached In Red Wine	Turmeric-Spiced Peach Compote	Pecan Nut & Pumpkin Pie
Sun	Key Lime Pie	Rice Pudding	Instant Pot Carrot Cardamom Cake	Instant Pot Baked Lemongrass and Black Peppercorn Pineapples

Menu For Month 2

	Week 1	Week 2	Week 3	Week 4
Mon	Spicy Citrus Beef	Marinara Beef Meatballs	Classic Beef Stew with Mushrooms and Peas	Instant Pot Beef Crock Roast
Tue	Beef and Rosemary Stew With Stir Fried Vegetables	Hungarian Beef Goulash	Beef and Rosemary Stew With Stir Fried Vegetables	South East Asian Beef Ribs and White Radish Stew
Wen	Instant Pot Oatmeal Beef Meatballs	Beef and Rosemary Stew With Stir Fried Vegetables	Spicy Citrus Beef	Classic Beef Stew with Mushrooms and Peas
Thu	Classic Beef Stew with Mushrooms and Peas	Instant Pot Beef Crock Roast	Balsamic & Rosemary Roast Beef	Raised Beef Ribs
Fri	Balsamic & Rosemary Roast Beef	South East Asian Beef Ribs and White Radish Stew	Instant Pot Oatmeal Beef Meatballs	Marinara Beef Meatballs
Sat	Instant Pot Carrot Cardamom Cake	All Haven Gooey Cake	Instant Pot Baked Lemongrass and Black Peppercorn Pineapples	Rice Pudding
Sun	Turmeric-Spiced Peach Compote	Key Lime Pie	Pecan Nut & Pumpkin Pie	Almond Barley and Snow Fungus Pudding

	Week 1	Week 2	Week 3	Week 4
Menu For Month 3				
Mon	Chicken Santa Fe Style	Instant Pot Roasted Tandoori Chicken	Sweet and Spicy Three Cups Chicken	Honey, Mustard & Lemon Chicken
Tue	Chicken, Butternut & Apple Stew	Poached Chicken in Coconut and Lime Cream Sauce	Sweet Honey and Lime Barbecue Chicken	Chicken Tandoori
Wen	Garlic & Lime Chicken	Chicken Adobo with Orange Salsa	Instant Pot Chicken Hainanese	Poached Chicken in Coconut and Lime Cream Sauce
Thu	Honey, Mustard & Lemon Chicken	Instant Pot Stuffed Chicken Breast	Poached Chicken in Coconut and Lime Cream Sauce	Spicy Five Peppers Hot Chicken Wings
Fri	Maple & Sesame Chicken	Spicy Five Peppers Hot Chicken Wings	Tamarind and Lemongrass Braised Chicken	Sweet Honey and Lime Barbecue Chicken
Sat	Instant Pot Carrot Cardamom Cake	All Haven Gooey Cake	Instant Pot Baked Lemongrass and Black Peppercorn Pineapples	Instant Pot Carrot Cardamom Cake
Sun	Key Lime Pie	Pears Poached In Red Wine	Rice Pudding	Turmeric-Spiced Peach Compote

	Week 1	Week 2	Week 3	Week 4
Menu For Month 4				
Mon	Garlic & Lime Chicken	Instant Pot Chicken Hainanese	Chicken Adobo with Orange Salsa	Honey, Mustard & Lemon Chicken
Tue	Maple & Sesame Chicken	Tamarind and Lemongrass Braised Chicken	Instant Pot Roasted Tandoori Chicken	Chicken Tandoori
Wen	Instant Pot Roasted Tandoori Chicken	Spicy Five Peppers Hot Chicken Wings	Maple & Sesame Chicken	Poached Chicken in Coconut and Lime Cream Sauce
Thu	Chicken Adobo with Orange Salsa	Poached Chicken in Coconut and Lime Cream Sauce	Garlic & Lime Chicken	Instant Pot Stuffed Chicken Breast
Fri	Spicy Five Peppers Hot Chicken Wings	Sweet Honey and Lime Barbecue Chicken	Chicken Santa Fe Style	Sweet and Spicy Soy Roast Chicken
Sat	Cassava and Sweet Potatoes Pudding with Coconut Milk Sauce	All Haven Gooey Cake	Chocolate Chip and Cocoa Pudding	Key Lime Pie
Sun	Pecan Nut & Pumpkin Pie	Instant Pot Baked Lemongrass and Black Peppercorn Pineapples	Instant Pot Carrot Cardamom Cake	Turmeric-Spiced Peach Compote

Menu For Month 5

	Week 1	Week 2	Week 3	Week 4
Mon	Turkey Breast with Fennel	Red Coconut Curry Turkey	Instant Pot Turkey Mole Poblano	Turkey Wings with Cranberries & Pecan Nuts
Tue	Turkey Legs with Porobello Mushrooms	Red Coconut Curry Turkey	Turkey with Sage and Thyme Rubs	Turkey Breast with Fennel
Wen	Instant Pot Turkey Mole Poblano	Braised Turkey Breast, Shiitake and Tofu	Moroccan Lemon, Lime and Olive Turkey Thighs	Turkey Legs with Porobello Mushrooms
Thu	Turkey Meatballs with Blueberries & Balsamic	Juniper and Citrus Turkey Leg Confit	Instant Pot Stuffed Turkey Breast Roast	Turkey & Bean Chili
Fri	Turkey Wings with Cranberries & Pecan Nuts	Instant Pot Turkey Mole Poblano	Red Coconut Curry Turkey	Turkey with Sage and Thyme Rubs
Sat	Rice Pudding	Instant Pot Carrot Cardamom Cake	Almond Coconut Rice Pudding with Almond Milk	Chocolate Chip and Cocoa Pudding
Sun	All Haven Gooey Cake	Almond Barley and Snow Fungus Pudding	Cherry Cheesecake	Pears Poached In Red Wine

Menu For Month 6

	Week 1	Week 2	Week 3	Week 4
Mon	Turkey Legs with Porobello Mushrooms	Turkey with Sage and Thyme Rubs	Turkey Breast with Fennel	Red Coconut Curry Turkey
Tue	Turkey Meatballs with Blueberries & Balsamic	Moroccan Lemon, Lime and Olive Turkey Thighs	Turkey Wings with Cranberries & Pecan Nuts	Moroccan Lemon, Lime and Olive Turkey Thighs
Wen	Instant Pot Turkey Mole Poblano	Juniper and Citrus Turkey Leg Confit	Turkey & Bean Chili	Turkey Breast with Fennel
Thu	Turkey Wings with Cranberries & Pecan Nuts	Red Coconut Curry Turkey	Juniper and Citrus Turkey Leg Confit	Turkey Legs with Porobello Mushrooms
Fri	Braised Turkey Breast, Shiitake and Tofu	Turkey & Bean Chili	Moroccan Lemon, Lime and Olive Turkey Thighs	Instant Pot Turkey Mole Poblano
Sat	Cherry Cheesecake	Rice Pudding	Turmeric-Spiced Peach Compote	Almond Barley and Snow Fungus Pudding
Sun	Turmeric-Spiced Peach Compote	Pecan Nut & Pumpkin Pie	Instant Pot Carrot Cardamom Cake	All Haven Gooey Cake

Menu For Month 7

	Week 1	Week 2	Week 3	Week 4
Mon	Clam Chowder	Steamed Cod Mediterranean Style	Exotic Cod Curry	Fusilli Pasta with Tuna & Olives
Tue	Fusilli Pasta with Tuna & Olives	Tomato Fish Curry	Tilapia and Shrimp Multigrain Paella	Salmon Poached In Ginger-Miso Broth
Wen	Mussels Normandy	Sour Cream and Greek Yogurt Salmon Dip	Mixed Seafood Moqueca	Steamed Cod Mediterranean Style
Thu	Shrimp Paella	Steam Banana and Coconut Tuna with Fruit Punch	Mussels Normandy	Sour Cream and Greek Yogurt Salmon Dip
Fri	Salmon Poached In Ginger-Miso Broth	Tilapia and Shrimp Multigrain Paella	Salmon Poached In Ginger-Miso Broth	Cod and Mussel Stew
Sat	Instant Pot Baked Lemongrass and Black Peppercorn Pineapples	Pecan Nut & Pumpkin Pie	Turmeric-Spiced Peach Compote	Key Lime Pie
Sun	Almond Coconut Rice Pudding with Almond Milk	Cassava and Sweet Potatoes Pudding with Coconut Milk Sauce	Chocolate Chip and Cocoa Pudding	Instant Pot Carrot Cardamom Cake

Menu For Month 8

	Week 1	Week 2	Week 3	Week 4
Mon	Fusilli Pasta with Tuna & Olives	Clam Chowder	Mussels Normandy	Tilapia and Shrimp Multigrain Paella
Tue	Salmon Poached In Ginger-Miso Broth	Tomato Fish Curry	Mixed Seafood Moqueca	Exotic Cod Curry
Wen	Steamed Cod Mediterranean Style	Fusilli Pasta with Tuna & Olives	Steam Banana and Coconut Tuna with Fruit Punch	Sour Cream and Greek Yogurt Salmon Dip
Thu	Sour Cream and Greek Yogurt Salmon Dip	Salmon Poached In Ginger-Miso Broth	Tomato Fish Curry	Cod and Mussel Stew
Fri	Tilapia and Shrimp Multigrain Paella	Steam Banana and Coconut Tuna with Fruit Punch	Fusilli Pasta with Tuna & Olives	Clam Chowder
Sat	Turmeric-Spiced Peach Compote	Almond Barley and Snow Fungus Pudding	Pecan Nut & Pumpkin Pie	Cherry Cheesecake
Sun	Key Lime Pie	Rice Pudding	Instant Pot Carrot Cardamom Cake	Instant Pot Baked Lemongrass and Black Peppercorn Pineapples

Menu For Month 9

	Week 1	Week 2	Week 3	Week 4
Mon	Mexican Style Pork Stuffed Bell Peppers	Instant Pot Ma Po Tofu	Mashed Beans with Sun-Dried Tomatoes, Bacon and Ham	Caribbean Pulled Pork Salad
Tue	Honey & Mustard Pork Chops	Instant Pot Pork Luau	Pineapple and Pepper Hawaiian Pork	Pork Sausage with Bell Peppers & Basil
Wen	Pork Carnitas	Instant Pot Deonjang Pork Spare Ribs	Pork Chops with Sweet and Savory Apple Sauce	Honey & Mustard Pork Chops
Thu	Pork Sausage with Bell Peppers & Basil	Caribbean Pulled Pork Salad	Pork Loin Roast With Caramelized Onions and Balsamic Vinegar	Mexican Style Pork Stuffed Bell Peppers
Fri	Pork Baby Back Ribs	Easy Instant Pot Egg and Cheese Bacon Strata	Smoky Butternut Squash Casserole	Pork Carnitas
Sat	Rice Pudding	All Haven Gooey Cake	Pecan Nut & Pumpkin Pie	Pears Poached In Red Wine
Sun	Turmeric-Spiced Peach Compote	Almond Barley and Snow Fungus Pudding	Cassava and Sweet Potatoes Pudding with Coconut Milk Sauce	Chocolate Chip and Cocoa Pudding

Menu For Month 10

	Week 1	Week 2	Week 3	Week 4
Mon	Honey & Mustard Pork Chops	Pineapple and Pepper Hawaiian Pork	Instant Pot Ma Po Tofu	Caribbean Pulled Pork Salad
Tue	Pork Sausage with Bell Peppers & Basil	Pork Loin Roast With Caramelized Onions and Balsamic Vinegar	Pork Baby Back Ribs	Mashed Beans with Sun-Dried Tomatoes, Bacon and Ham
Wen	Smoky Butternut Squash Casserole	Pork Chops with Sweet and Savory Apple Sauce	Pork Carnitas	Pork Loin Roast With Caramelized Onions and Balsamic Vinegar
Thu	Instant Pot Pork Luau	Mashed Beans with Sun-Dried Tomatoes, Bacon and Ham	Mexican Style Pork Stuffed Bell Peppers	Instant Pot Ma Po Tofu
Fri	Caribbean Pulled Pork Salad	Easy Instant Pot Egg and Cheese Bacon Strata	Pork Sausage with Bell Peppers & Basil	Instant Pot Pork Luau
Sat	Cherry Cheesecake	Instant Pot Carrot Cardamom Cake	Turmeric-Spiced Peach Compote	Chocolate Chip and Cocoa Pudding
Sun	Rice Pudding	Instant Pot Baked Lemongrass and Black Peppercorn Pineapples	All Haven Gooey Cake	Almond Coconut Rice Pudding with Almond Milk

Vegetarian Only

	Menu For Month 11			
	Week 1	Week 2	Week 3	Week 4
Mon	Bean and Chickpea Chili	Corn, Pinto and Quinoa Enchilada with Vegan Cheese	Spinach Ndole	Apple Cranberry Sauce With Orange Zest
Tue	Lentil, Broccoli & Okra Curry	Instant Pot Red Beans With Fruity Punch	Instant Pot Baked Provencales Tomatoe	Bean and Chickpea Chili
Wen	Penne All'arrabiata	Instant Pot Vegan Mushroom Lasagna	Linguini with Mixed Mushroom Ragout	Linguini with Mixed Mushroom Ragout
Thu	Linguini with Mixed Mushroom Ragout	Vegetarian Chickpea, Quinoa and Spinach Chili	Coconut and Chill Green Beans	Apple Cranberry Sauce With Orange Zest
Fri	Coconut and Chili Green Beans	Instant Pot Zucchini Shakshuka	Instant Pot Cauliflower and Chickpea Curry	Korean Eggplant and Rice Cake Stew
Sat	Instant Pot Carrot Cardamom Cake	Rice Pudding	All Haven Gooey Cake	Key Lime Pie
Sun	Chocolate Chip and Cocoa Pudding	Almond Barley and Snow Fungus Pudding	Turmeric-Spiced Peach Compote	Instant Pot Baked Lemongrass and Black Peppercorn Pineapples

	Menu For Month 12			
	Week 1	Week 2	Week 3	Week 4
Mon	Lentil, Broccoli & Okra Curry	Linguini with Mixed Mushroom Ragout.	Instant Pot Red Beans With Fruity Punch	Corn, Pinto and Quinoa Enchilada with Vegan Cheese
Tue	Instant Pot Zucchini Shakshuka	Instant Pot Cauliflower and Chickpea Curry	Apple Cranberry Sauce With Orange Zest	Instant Pot Vegan Mushroom Lasagna
Wen	Apple Cranberry Sauce With Orange Zest	Coconut and Chill Green Beans	Linguini with Mixed Mushroom Ragout	Instant Pot Zucchini Shakshuka
Thu	Instant Pot Red Beans With Fruity Punch	Instant Pot Baked Provencale Tomatoes	Lentil, Broccoli & Okra Curry	Spinach Ndole
Fri	Linguini with Mixed Mushroom Ragout	Korean Eggplant anc Rice Cake Stew	Penne All'arrabiata	Linguini with Mixed Mushroom Ragout.
Sat	Almond Coconut Rice Pudding with Almond Milk	Pears Poached In Red Wine	Pecan Nut & Pumpkin Pie	Chocolate Chip and Cocoa Pudding
Sun	Instant Pot Carrot Cardamom Cake	Rice Pudding	Key Lime Pie	Cherry Cheesecake

Menu For Month 13

	Week 1	Week 2	Week 3	Week 4
Mon	Butternut Squash Soup	Tomato & Basil Cream Soup	Irish Lamb Stew with Red Wine	Instant Pot Beef and Red Wine Stew
Tue	Collard Greens, Chorizo & Chicken Soup	Cream of Leek and Bacon Soup	Quinoa and Black Eyed Beans Chicken Soup	Beef Ribs, Kidney Beans, and Root Vegetables Stew
Wen	Corn & Bacon Chowder	Crab and Winter Bamboo Shoot Egg Drop Soup	Smoked Ham and Chicken Soup with Eggs	Instant Pot Roasted Tomato Gazpacho
Thu	Leek & Potato Soup	Instant Pot Roasted Tomato Gazpacho	Spicy Veggie and Tilapia Soup	Cream of Leek and Bacon Soup
Fri	Cream of Leek and Bacon Soup	Beef Ribs, Kidney Beans, and Root Vegetables Stew	Chicken, Tofu and Mixed Vegetables Clear Soup	Tomato & Basil Cream Soup
Sat	Pecan Nut & Pumpkin Pie	Chocolate Chip and Cocoa Pudding	Rice Pudding	Cherry Cheesecake
Sun	Almond Barley and Snow Fungus Pudding	Turmeric-Spiced Peach Compote	Cassava and Sweet Potatoes Pudding with Coconut Milk Sauce	Key Lime Pie

Menu For Month 14

	Week 1	Week 2	Week 3	Week 4
Mon	Collard Greens, Chorizo & Chicken Soup	Quinoa and Black Eyed Beans Chicken Soup	Irish Lamb Stew with Red Wine	Leek & Potato Soup
Tue	Leek & Potato Soup	Spicy Veggie and Tilapia Soup	Beef Ribs, Kidney Beans, and Root Vegetables Stew	Collard Greens, Chorizo & Chicken Soup
Wen	Crab and Winter Bamboo Shoot Egg Drop Soup	Classic Beef Stew with Mushroom and Peas	Crab and Winter Bamboo Shoot Egg Drop Soup	Butternut Squash Soup
Thu	Cream of Leek and Bacon Soup	Instant Pot Beef and Red Wine Stew	Tomato & Basil Cream Soup	Crab and Winter Bamboo Shoot Egg Drop Soup
Fri	Instant Pot Roasted Tomato Gazpacho	Chicken, Tofu and Mixed Vegetables Clear Soup	Cream of Leek and Bacon Soup	Beef Ribs, Kidney Beans, and Root Vegetables Stew
Sat	Instant Pot Baked Lemongrass and Black Peppercorn Pineapples	All Haven Gooey Cake	Turmeric-Spiced Peach Compote	Cherry Cheesecake
Sun	Pears Poached In Red Wine	Instant Pot Carrot Cardamom Cake	Rice Pudding	Almond Barley and Snow Fungus Pudding

Menu For Month 15

	Week 1	Week 2	Week 3	Week 4
Mon	Balsamic & Rosemary Roast Beef	Butternut Squash Soup	Fusilli Pasta with Tuna & Olives	Spicy Citrus Beef
Tue	Chicken Santa Fe Style	Instant Pot Beef Chili Stuffed Peppers	Honey & Mustard Pork Chops	Garlic & Lime Chicken
Wen	Turkey Breast with Fennel	Port Wine Lamb Shanks	Lentil, Broccoli & Okra Curry	Turkey Wings with Cranberries & Pecan Nuts
Thu	Clam Chowder	Marinara Beef Meatballs	Collard Greens, Chorizo & Chicken Soup	Cod and Mussel Stew
Fri	Mexican Style Pork Stuffed Bell Peppers	Chicken, Butternut & Apple Stew	Instant Pot Potato and Tofu Stuffed Chilies	Pork Carnitas
Sat	Bean and Chickpea Chili	Turkey Legs with Porobello Mushrooms	Port Wine Lamb Shanks	Penne All'arrabiata
Sun	Pears Poached In Red Wine	Chocolate Chip and Cocoa Pudding	Turmeric-Spiced Peach Compote	Almond Coconut Rice Pudding with Almond Milk

Menu For Month 16

	Week 1	Week 2	Week 3	Week 4
Mon	Corn & Bacon Chowder	Salmon Poached In Ginger-Miso Broth	Raised Beef Ribs	Cream of Leek and Bacon Soup
Tue	Butternut, Black Bean & Sweet Potato Chili	Pork Sausage with Bell Peppers & Basil	Maple & Sesame Chicken	Instant Pot Beef Chili Stuffed Peppers
Wen	Port Wine Lamb Shanks	Linguini with Mixed Mushroom Ragout	Turkey & Bean Chili	Port Wine Lamb Shanks
Thu	Hungarian Beef Goulash	Leek & Potato Soup	Mixed Seafood Moqueca	Beef and Rosemary Stew With Stir Fried Vegetables
Fri	Honey, Mustard & Lemon Chicken	Paprika Chili Chicken	Pork Baby Back Ribs	Chicken Tandoori
Sat	Turkey Meatballs with Blueberries & Balsamic	Port Wine Lamb Shanks	Coconut and Chili Green Beans	Red Coconut Curry Turkey
Sun	Cassava and Sweet Potatoes Pudding with Coconut Milk Sauce	Instant Pot Carrot Cardamom Cake	Rice Pudding	Cherry Cheesecake

Menu For Month 17

	Week 1	Week 2	Week 3	Week 4
Mon	Steamed Cod Mediterranean Style	Instant Pot Beef Crock Roast	Tomato & Basil Cream Soup	Tomato Fish Curry
Tue	Smoky Butternut Squash Casserole	Instant Pot Roasted Tandoori Chicken	Instant Pot Potato and Tofu Stuffed Chilies	Instant Pot Pork Luau
Wen	Coconut and Chili Green Beans	Red Coconut Curry Turkey	Port Wine Lamb Shanks	Corn, Pinto and Quinoa Enchilada with Vegan Cheese
Thu	Crab and Winter Bamboo Shoot Egg Drop Soup	Steamed Cod Mediterranean Style	Instant Pot Oatmeal Beef Meatballs	Cream of Leek and Bacon Soup
Fri	Instant Pot Potato and Tofu Stuffed Chilies	Instant Pot Ma Po Tofu	Chicken Adobo with Orange Salsa	Paprika Chili Chicken
Sat	Port Wine Lamb Shanks	Apple Cranberry Sauce With Orange Zest	Instant Pot Turkey Mole Poblano	Steamed Cod Mediterranean Style
Sun	Almond Coconut Rice Pudding with Almond Milk	Chocolate Chip and Cocoa Pudding	Instant Pot Carrot Cardamom Cake	All Haven Gooey Cake

Menu For Month 18

	Week 1	Week 2	Week 3	Week 4
Mon	Port Wine Lamb Shanks	Turkey with Sage and Thyme Rubs	Pork Chops with Sweet and Savory Apple Sauce	Chicken, Tofu and Mixed Vegetables Clear Soup
Tue	Paprika Chili Chicken	Instant Pot Roasted Tandoori Chicken	Cod and Mussel Stew	Linguini with Mixed Mushroom Ragout.
Wen	Instant Pot Beef and Red Wine Stew	Classic Beef Stew with Mushrooms and Peas	Instant Pot Stuffed Turkey Breast Roast	Pineapple and Pepper Hawaiian Pork
Thu	Instant Pot Cauliflower and Chickpea Curry	Instant Pot Potato and Tofu Stuffed Chilies	Tamarind and Lemongrass Braised Chicken	Tilapia and Shrimp Multigrain Paella
Fri	Pork Loin Roast With Caramelized Onions and Balsamic Vinegar	Chicken, Tofu and Mixed Vegetables Clear Soup	South East Asian Beef Ribs and White Radish Stew	Moroccan Lemon, Lime and Olive Turkey Thighs
Sat	Exotic Cod Curry	Coconut and Chill Green Beans	Instant Pot Beef Chili Stuffed Peppers	Poached Chicken in Coconut and Lime Cream Sauce
Sun	Almond Barley and Snow Fungus Pudding	Turmeric-Spiced Peach Compote	Instant Pot Baked Lemongrass and Black Peppercorn Pineapples	Instant Pot Carrot Cardamom Cake

Menu For Month 19

	Week 1	Week 2	Week 3	Week 4
Mon	Instant Pot Oatmeal Beef Meatballs	Spicy Veggie and Tilapia Soup	Sour Cream and Greek Yogurt Salmon Dip	Salmon Poached In Ginger-Miso Broth
Tue	Instant Pot Chicken Hainanese	Butternut, Black Bean & Sweet Potato Chili	Juniper and Citrus Turkey Leg Confit	Instant Pot Deonjang Pork Spare Ribs
Wen	Braised Turkey Breast, Shiitake and Tofu	Port Wine Lamb Shanks	Sweet Honey and Lime Barbecue Chicken	Corn, Pinto and Quinoa Enchilada with Vegan Cheese
Thu	Steam Banana and Coconut Tuna with Fruit Punch	Smoked Ham and Chicken Soup with Eggs	Beef and Rosemary Stew With Stir Fried Vegetables	Cream of Leek and Bacon Soup
Fri	Mashed Beans with Sun-Dried Tomatoes, Bacon and Ham	Korean Eggplant and Rice Cake Stew	Instant Pot Stuffed Chicken Breast	Paprika Chili Chicken
Sat	Instant Pot Baked Provencale Tomatoes	Easy Instant Pot Egg and Cheese Bacon Strata	Red Coconut Curry Turkey	Port Wine Lamb Shanks
Sun	Rice Pudding	Key Lime Pie	Cherry Cheesecake	Chocolate Chip and Cocoa Pudding

Menu For Month 20

	Week 1	Week 2	Week 3	Week 4
Mon	Instant Pot Beef Chili Stuffed Peppers	Sweet and Spicy Soy Roast Chicken	Lentil, Broccoli & Okra Curry	Pork Loin Roast With Caramelized Onions and Balsamic Vinegar
Tue	Quinoa and Black Eyed Beans Chicken Soup	Beef and Rosemary Stew With Stir Fried Vegetables	Butternut Squash Soup	Steamed Cod Mediterranean Style
Wen	Korean Eggplant and Rice Cake Stew	Chicken, Butternut & Apple Stew	Instant Pot Potato and Tofu Stuffed Chilies	Juniper and Citrus Turkey Leg Confit
Thu	Easy Instant Pot Egg and Cheese Bacon Strata	Turkey Breast with Fennel	Port Wine Lamb Shanks	Tamarind and Lemongrass Braised Chicken
Fri	Sour Cream and Greek Yogurt Salmon Dip	Fusilli Pasta with Tuna & Olives	Spicy Veggie and Tilapia Soup	Instant Pot Beef Crock Roast
Sat	Instant Pot Stuffed Turkey Breast Roast	Mexican Style Pork Stuffed Bell Peppers	Linguini with Mixed Mushroom Ragout.	Instant Pot Chicken Hainanese
Sun	Almond Coconut Rice Pudding with Almond Milk	Turmeric-Spiced Peach Compote	Cassava and Sweet Potatoes Pudding with Coconut Milk Sauce	Turmeric-Spiced Peach Compote

Menu For Month 21

	Week 1	Week 2	Week 3	Week 4
Mon	Beef and Rosemary Stew With Stir Fried Vegetables	Butternut Squash Soup	Cod and Mussel Stew	Mixed Seafood Moqueca
Tue	Chicken Santa Fe Style	Butternut, Black Bean & Sweet Potato Chili	Turkey Meatballs with Blueberries & Balsamic	Instant Pot Pork Luau
Wen	Braised Turkey Breast, Shiitake and Tofu	Port Wine Lamb Shanks	Instant Pot Roasted Tandoori Chicken	Corn, Pinto and Quinoa Enchilada with Vegan Cheese
Thu	Clam Chowder	Quinoa and Black Eyed Beans Chicken Soup	Raised Beef Ribs	Crab and Winter Bamboo Shoot Egg Drop Soup
Fri	Instant Pot Ma Po Tofu	Instant Pot Cauliflower and Chickpea Curry	Maple & Sesame Chicken	Instant Pot Beef Chili Stuffed Peppers
Sat	Instant Pot Red Beans With Fruity Punch	Mashed Beans with Sun-Dried Tomatoes, Bacon and Ham	Turkey Wings with Cranberries & Pecan Nuts	Port Wine Lamb Shanks
Sun	Instant Pot Baked Lemongrass and Black Peppercorn Pineapples	Almond Barley and Snow Fungus Pudding	Pears Poached In Red Wine	Cherry Cheesecake

Menu For Month 22

	Week 1	Week 2	Week 3	Week 4
Mon	Marinara Beef Meatballs	Collard Greens, Chorizo & Chicken Soup	Pork Carnitas	Instant Pot Beef and Red Wine Stew
Tue	Tamarind and Lemongrass Braised Chicken	Butternut, Black Bean & Sweet Potato Chili	Linguini with Mixed Mushroom Ragout.	Bean and Chickpea Chili
Wen	Turkey Legs with Porobello Mushrooms	Instant Pot Oatmeal Beef Meatballs	Corn & Bacon Chowder	Pork Loin Roast With Caramelized Onions and Balsamic Vinegar
Thu	Cod and Mussel Stew	Garlic & Lime Chicken	Port Wine Lamb Shanks	Exotic Cod Curry
Fri	Honey & Mustard Pork Chops	Turkey Wings with Cranberries & Pecan Nuts	Butternut, Black Bean & Sweet Potato Chili	Turkey Breast with Fennel
Sat	Coconut and Chill Green Beans	Tilapia and Shrimp Multigrain Paella	Instant Pot Beef Chili Stuffed Peppers	Instant Pot Roasted Tandoori Chicken
Sun	Pecan Nut & Pumpkin Pie	Almond Coconut Rice Pudding with Almond Milk	Turmeric-Spiced Peach Compote	Pears Poached In Red Wine

Menu For Month 23

	Week 1	Week 2	Week 3	Week 4
Mon	Balsamic & Rosemary Roast Beef	Instant Pot Roasted Tomato Gazpacho	Red Coconut Curry Turkey	Honey and Garlic Pork Roast With Baked Beans and Sour Cream
Tue	Poached Chicken in Coconut and Lime Cream Sauce	Butternut, Black Bean & Sweet Potato Chili	Chicken Tandoori	Instant Pot Baked Provencale Tomatoes
Wen	Instant Pot Turkey Mole Poblano	Cream of Leek and Bacon Soup	Hungarian Beef Goulash	Quinoa and Black Eyed Beans Chicken Soup
Thu	Tomato Fish Curry	Coconut and Chili Green Beans	Tamarind and Lemongrass Braised Chicken	Paprika Chili Chicken
Fri	Instant Pot Ma Po Tofu	Pork Baby Back Ribs	Instant Pot Stuffed Turkey Breast Roast	Port Wine Lamb Shanks
Sat	Instant Pot Red Beans With Fruity Punch	Mixed Seafood Moqueca	Tilapia and Shrimp Multigrain Paella	Cream of Leek and Bacon Soup
Sun	Key Lime Pie	Pecan Nut & Pumpkin Pie	Almond Coconut Rice Pudding with Almond Milk	Instant Pot Carrot Cardamom Cake

Menu For Month 24

	Week 1	Week 2	Week 3	Week 4
Mon	Raised Beef Ribs	Instant Pot Roasted Tomato Gazpacho	Mashed Beans with Sun-Dried Tomatoes, Bacon and Ham	Turkey Legs with Porobello Mushrooms
Tue	Chicken Santa Fe Style	Instant Pot Beef Chili Stuffed Peppers	Sour Cream and Greek Yogurt Salmon Dip	Exotic Cod Curry
Wen	Red Coconut Curry Turkey	Port Wine Lamb Shanks	Instant Pot Turkey Mole Poblano	Honey & Mustard Pork Chops
Thu	Clam Chowder	Paprika Chili Chicken	Spicy Five Peppers Hot Chicken Wings	Instant Pot Cauliflower and Chickpea Curry
Fri	Instant Pot Pork Luau	Classic Beef Stew with Mushroom and Peas	Spicy Citrus Beef	Collard Greens, Chorizo & Chicken Soup
Sat	Bean and Chickpea Chili	Linguini with Mixed Mushroom Ragout.	Chicken Santa Fe Style	Paprika Chili Chicken
Sun	Turmeric-Spiced Peach Compote	Instant Pot Carrot Cardamom Cake	Instant Pot Baked Lemongrass and Black Peppercorn Pineapples	Key Lime Pie

Menu For Month 25

	Week 1	Week 2	Week 3	Week 4
Mon	Port Wine Lamb Shanks	Turkey Breast with Fennel	Lentil, Broccoli & Okra Curry	Paprika Chili Chicken
Tue	Instant Pot Beef Chili Stuffed Peppers	Chicken Santa Fe Style	Pork Carnitas	Cream of Leek and Bacon Soup
Wen	Clam Chowder	Balsamic & Rosemary Roast Beef	Cod and Mussel Stew	Coconut and Chili Green Beans
Thu	Butternut Squash Soup	Instant Pot Potato and Tofu Stuffed Chilies	Turkey Wings with Cranberries & Pecan Nuts	Instant Pot Pork Luau
Fri	Bean and Chickpea Chili	Cream of Leek and Bacon Soup	Garlic & Lime Chicken	Mixed Seafood Moqueca
Sat	Mexican Style Pork Stuffed Bell Peppers	Collard Greens, Chorizo & Chicken Soup	Spicy Citrus Beef	Red Coconut Curry Turkey
Sun	Cassava and Sweet Potatoes Pudding with Coconut Milk Sauce	Turmeric-Spiced Peach Compote	Almond Coconut Rice Pudding with Almond Milk	Almond Barley and Snow Fungus Pudding

Menu For Month 26

	Week 1	Week 2	Week 3	Week 4
Mon	South East Asian Beef Ribs and White Radish Stew	Classic Beef Stew with Mushroom and Peas	Sour Cream and Greek Yogurt Salmon Dip	Port Wine Lamb Shanks
Tue	Garlic & Lime Chicken	Butternut, Black Bean & Sweet Potato Chili	Mexican Style Pork Stuffed Bell Peppers	Beef and Rosemary Stew With Stir Fried Vegetables
Wen	Instant Pot Stuffed Turkey Breast Roast	Port Wine Lamb Shanks	Corn, Pinto and Quinoa Enchilada with Vegan Cheese	Instant Pot Stuffed Chicken Breast
Thu	Cod and Mussel Stew	Spicy Citrus Beef	Butternut Squash Soup	Red Coconut Curry Turkey
Fri	Pork Chops with Sweet and Savory Apple Sauce	Sweet and Spicy Three Cups Chicken	Pecan Nut & Pumpkin Pie	Steamed Cod Mediterranean Style
Sat	Penne All'arrabiata	Turkey Wings with Cranberries & Pecan Nuts	Instant Pot Beef Chili Stuffed Peppers	Caribbean Pulled Pork Salad
Sun	Pecan Nut & Pumpkin Pie	Rice Pudding	Almond Barley and Snow Fungus Pudding	Chocolate Chip and Cocoa Pudding

Menu For Month 27

	Week 1	Week 2	Week 3	Week 4
Mon	Instant Pot Beef Crock Roast	Tomato & Basil Cream Soup	Steamed Cod Mediterranean Style	Crab and Winter Bamboo Shoot Egg Drop Soup
Tue	Honey, Mustard & Lemon Chicken	Instant Pot Potato and Tofu Stuffed Chilies	Instant Pot Turkey Mole Poblano	Coconut and Chill Green Beans
Wen	Turkey & Bean Chili	Port Wine Lamb Shanks	Chicken Adobo with Orange Salsa	Pork Baby Back Ribs
Thu	Sour Cream and Greek Yogurt Salmon Dip	Quinoa and Black Eyed Beans Chicken Soup	Raised Beef Ribs	Salmon Poached In Ginger-Miso Broth
Fri	Smoky Butternut Squash Casserole	Linguini with Mixed Mushroom Ragout	Port Wine Lamb Shanks	Instant Pot Turkey Mole Poblano
Sat	Coconut and Chili Green Beans	Honey and Garlic Pork Roast With Baked Beans and Sour Cream	Instant Pot Beef Chili Stuffed Peppers	Maple & Sesame Chicken
Sun	Turmeric-Spiced Peach Compote	Turmeric-Spiced Peach Compote	Cherry Cheesecake	Almond Coconut Rice Pudding with Almond Milk

Menu For Month 28

	Week 1	Week 2	Week 3	Week 4
Mon	Spicy Citrus Beef	Instant Pot Zucchini Shakshuka	Red Coconut Curry Turkey	Exotic Cod Curry
Tue	Spicy Five Peppers Hot Chicken Wings	Instant Pot Roasted Tomato Gazpacho	Sweet and Spicy Soy Roast Chicken	Pork Loin Roast With Caramelized Onions and Balsamic Vinegar
Wen	Braised Turkey Breast, Shiitake and Tofu	Butternut, Black Bean & Sweet Potato Chili	Instant Pot Beef Crock Roast	Instant Pot Cauliflower and Chickpea Curry
Thu	Tomato Fish Curry	Port Wine Lamb Shanks	Classic Beef Stew with Mushrooms and Peas	Instant Pot Beef and Red Wine Stew
Fri	Pork Carnitas	Coconut and Chili Green Beans	Instant Pot Roasted Tandoori Chicken	Instant Pot Potato and Tofu Stuffed Chilies
Sat	Mashed Beans with Sun-Dried Tomatoes, Bacon and Ham	Steamed Cod Mediterranean Style	Turkey with Sage and Thyme Rubs	Instant Pot Beef Crock Roast
Sun	Instant Pot Carrot Cardamom Cake	Turmeric-Spiced Peach Compote	Almond Barley and Snow Fungus Pudding	All Haven Gooey Cake

No Pork

	Menu For Month 29			
	Week 1	**Week 2**	**Week 3**	**Week 4**
Mon	Balsamic & Rosemary Roast Beef	Instant Pot Potato and Tofu Stuffed Chilies	Spinach Ndole	Fusilli Pasta with Tuna & Olives
Tue	Instant Pot Roasted Tandoori Chicken	Port Wine Lamb Shanks	Spicy Veggie and Tilapia Soup	Turkey Meatballs with Blueberries & Balsamic
Wen	Turkey & Bean Chili	Instant Pot Oatmeal Beef Meatballs	Paprika Chili Chicken	Instant Pot Roasted Tandoori Chicken
Thu	Steam Banana and Coconut Tuna with Fruit Punch	Sweet Honey and Lime Barbecue Chicken	Port Wine Lamb Shanks	Marinara Beef Meatballs
Fri	Instant Pot Red Beans With Fruity Punch	Moroccan Lemon, Lime and Olive Turkey Thighs	Leek & Potato Soup	Tilapia and Shrimp Multigrain Paella
Sat	Cream of Leek and Bacon Soup	Steam Banana and Coconut Tuna with Fruit Punch	Lentil, Broccoli & Okra Curry	Irish Lamb Stew with Red Wine
Sun	Instant Pot Baked Lemongrass and Black Peppercorn Pineapples	Cassava and Sweet Potatoes Pudding with Coconut Milk Sauce	All Haven Gooey Cake	Pears Poached In Red Wine

	Menu For Month 30			
	Week 1	**Week 2**	**Week 3**	**Week 4**
Mon	Port Wine Lamb Shanks	Chicken Santa Fe Style	Instant Pot Stuffed Turkey Breast Roast	Salmon Poached In Ginger-Miso Broth
Tue	Instant Pot Beef Chili Stuffed Peppers	Balsamic & Rosemary Roast Beef	Tamarind and Lemongrass Braised Chicken	Linguini with Mixed Mushroom Ragout
Wen	Butternut Squash Soup	Butternut, Black Bean & Sweet Potato Chili	South East Asian Beef Ribs and White Radish Stew	Cream of Leek and Bacon Soup
Thu	Bean and Chickpea Chili	Classic Beef Stew with Mushroom and Peas	Hungarian Beef Goulash	Paprika Chili Chicken
Fri	Clam Chowder	Coconut and Chill Green Beans	Honey, Mustard & Lemon Chicken	Instant Pot Zucchini Shakshuka
Sat	Turkey Breast with Fennel	Cod and Mussel Stew	Turkey Meatballs with Blueberries & Balsamic	Mixed Seafood Moqueca
Sun	Cherry Cheesecake	Rice Pudding	Chocolate Chip and Cocoa Pudding	Instant Pot Carrot Cardamom Cake

Menu For Month 31

	Week 1	Week 2	Week 3	Week 4
Mon	Honey, Mustard & Lemon Chicken	Pork Carnitas	Balsamic & Rosemary Roast Beef	Bean and Chickpea Chili
Tue	Poached Chicken in Coconut and Lime Cream Sauce	Pineapple and Pepper Hawaiian Pork	Classic Beef Stew with Mushrooms and Peas	Butternut Squash Soup
Wen	Turkey Meatballs with Blueberries & Balsamic	Coconut and Chili Green Beans	Chicken Santa Fe Style	Crab and Winter Bamboo Shoot Egg Drop Soup
Thu	Instant Pot Stuffed Turkey Breast Roast	Corn & Bacon Chowder	Turkey Breast with Fennel	Instant Pot Beef Chili Stuffed Peppers
Fri	Tomato Fish Curry	Chicken, Tofu and Mixed Vegetables Clear Soup	Clam Chowder	Port Wine Lamb Shanks
Sat	Tilapia and Shrimp Multigrain Paella	Instant Pot Potato and Tofu Stuffed Chilies	Mexican Style Pork Stuffed Bell Peppers	Coconut and Chili Green Beans
Sun	Pears Poached In Red Wine	Turmeric-Spiced Peach Compote	Rice Pudding	Pecan Nut & Pumpkin Pie

Menu For Month 32

	Week 1	Week 2	Week 3	Week 4
Mon	Classic Beef Stew with Mushrooms and Peas	Instant Pot Beef and Red Wine Stew	Tilapia and Shrimp Multigrain Paella	Honey, Mustard & Lemon Chicken
Tue	Instant Pot Roasted Tandoori Chicken	Paprika Chili Chicken	Pineapple and Pepper Hawaiian Pork	Turkey Meatballs with Blueberries & Balsamic
Wen	Turkey with Sage and Thyme Rubs	Port Wine Lamb Shanks	Linguini with Mixed Mushroom Ragout	Salmon Poached In Ginger-Miso Broth
Thu	Exotic Cod Curry	Instant Pot Oatmeal Beef Meatballs	Chicken, Tofu and Mixed Vegetables Clear Soup	Pork Sausage with Bell Peppers & Basil
Fri	Pork Loin Roast With Caramelized Onions and Balsamic Vinegar	Poached Chicken in Coconut and Lime Cream Sauce	Instant Pot Potato and Tofu Stuffed Chilies	Linguini with Mixed Mushroom Ragout
Sat	Instant Pot Zucchini Shakshuka	Moroccan Lemon, Lime and Olive Turkey Thighs	Hungarian Beef Goulash	Leek & Potato Soup
Sun	Rice Pudding	Instant Pot Baked Lemongrass and Black Peppercorn Pineapples	Cassava and Sweet Potatoes Pudding with Coconut Milk Sauce	Pecan Nut & Pumpkin Pie

Menu For Month 33

	Week 1	Week 2	Week 3	Week 4
Mon	Hungarian Beef Goulash	Instant Pot Roasted Tomato Gazpacho	Tomato Fish Curry	Spicy Citrus Beef
Tue	Poached Chicken in Coconut and Lime Cream Sauce	Butternut, Black Bean & Sweet Potato Chili	Easy Instant Pot Egg and Cheese Bacon Strata	Chicken Tandoori
Wen	Instant Pot Turkey Mole Poblano	Port Wine Lamb Shanks	Vegetarian Chickpea, Quinoa and Spinach Chili	Turkey & Bean Chili
Thu	Tomato Fish Curry	Instant Pot Oatmeal Beef Meatballs	Instant Pot Roasted Tomato Gazpacho	Salmon Poached In Ginger-Miso Broth
Fri	Instant Pot Ma Po Tofu	Sweet and Spicy Soy Roast Chicken	Instant Pot Beef Chili Stuffed Peppers	Pork Baby Back Ribs
Sat	Instant Pot Red Beans With Fruity Punch	Juniper and Citrus Turkey Leg Confit	Instant Pot Turkey Mole Poblano	Coconut and Chili Green Beans
Sun	Instant Pot Carrot Cardamom Cake	Instant Pot Carrot Cardamom Cake	Chocolate Chip and Cocoa Pudding	Key Lime Pie

Menu For Month 34

	Week 1	Week 2	Week 3	Week 4
Mon	Leek & Potato Soup	Tomato Fish Curry	Instant Pot Oatmeal Beef Meatballs	Smoked Ham and Chicken Soup with Eggs
Tue	Butternut, Black Bean & Sweet Potato Chili	Caribbean Pulled Pork Salad	Spicy Five Peppers Hot Chicken Wings	Port Wine Lamb Shanks
Wen	Port Wine Lamb Shanks	Smoked Ham and Chicken Soup with Eggs	Red Coconut Curry Turkey	Coconut and Chill Green Beans
Thu	Hungarian Beef Goulash	Spinach Ndole	Tomato Fish Curry	Honey & Mustard Pork Chops
Fri	Sweet and Spicy Soy Roast Chicken	Leek & Potato Soup	Instant Pot Deonjang Pork Spare Ribs	Salmon Poached In Ginger-Miso Broth
Sat	Turkey & Bean Chili	Instant Pot Beef Chili Stuffed Peppers	Instant Pot Red Beans With Fruity Punch	Turkey Meatballs with Blueberries & Balsamic
Sun	Instant Pot Carrot Cardamom Cake	Instant Pot Carrot Cardamom Cake	Almond Barley and Snow Fungus Pudding	Instant Pot Carrot Cardamom Cake

Menu For Month 35

	Week 1	Week 2	Week 3	Week 4
Mon	Sweet and Spicy Three Cups Chicken	Instant Pot Zucchini Shakshuka	Hungarian Beef Goulash	Instant Pot Potato and Tofu Stuffed Chilies
Tue	Honey, Mustard & Lemon Chicken	Instant Pot Roasted Tomato Gazpacho	Salmon Poached In Ginger-Miso Broth	Quinoa and Black Eyed Beans Chicken Soup
Wen	Raised Beef Ribs	Paprika Chili Chicken	Instant Pot Ma Po Tofu	Instant Pot Vegan Mushroom Lasagna
Thu	Moroccan Lemon, Lime and Olive Turkey Thighs	Port Wine Lamb Shanks	Coconut and Chili Green Beans	Caribbean Pulled Pork Salad
Fri	Sour Cream and Greek Yogurt Salmon Dip	Turkey Meatballs with Blueberries & Balsamic	Instant Pot Cauliflower and Chickpea Curry	Steam Banana and Coconut Tuna with Fruit Punch
Sat	Instant Pot Pork Luau	Spicy Five Peppers Hot Chicken Wings	Beef Ribs, Kidney Beans, and Root Vegetables Stew	Instant Pot Turkey Mole Poblano
Sun	Cassava and Sweet Potatoes Pudding with Coconut Milk Sauce	Instant Pot Carrot Cardamom Cake	Almond Coconut Rice Pudding with Almond Milk	Rice Pudding

Menu For Month 36

	Week 1	Week 2	Week 3	Week 4
Mon	Instant Pot Beef Crock Roast	Coconut and Chill Green Beans	Turkey & Bean Chili	Instant Pot Roasted Tandoori Chicken
Tue	Honey, Mustard & Lemon Chicken	Leek & Potato Soup	Steamed Cod Mediterranean Style	Braised Turkey Breast, Shiitake and Tofu
Wen	Red Coconut Curry Turkey	Port Wine Lamb Shanks	Easy Instant Pot Egg and Cheese Bacon Strata	Tomato Fish Curry
Thu	Tilapia and Shrimp Multigrain Paella	Instant Pot Potato and Tofu Stuffed Chilies	Coconut and Chili Green Beans	Caribbean Pulled Pork Salad
Fri	Pork Carnitas	South East Asian Beef Ribs and White Radish Stew	Creamy Corn and Asparagus Chicken Soup	Coconut and Chili Green Beans
Sat	Pineapple and Pepper Hawaiian Pork	Instant Pot Roasted Tandoori Chicken	Butternut, Black Bean & Sweet Potato Chili	Instant Pot Roasted Tomato Gazpacho
Sun	Key Lime Pie	Instant Pot Carrot Cardamom Cake	Chocolate Chip and Cocoa Pudding	Cherry Cheesecake

Menu For Month 37

	Week 1	Week 2	Week 3	Week 4
Mon	Balsamic & Rosemary Roast Beef	Korean Eggplant and Rice Cake Stew	Red Coconut Curry Turkey	Collard Greens, Chorizo & Chicken Soup
Tue	Instant Pot Oatmeal Beef Meatballs	Tomato & Basil Cream Soup	Sour Cream and Greek Yogurt Salmon Dip	Coconut and Chili Green Beans
Wen	Instant Pot Roasted Tandoori Chicken	Instant Pot Potato and Tofu Stuffed Chilies	Mashed Beans with Sun-Dried Tomatoes, Bacon and Ham	Honey & Mustard Pork Chops
Thu	Turkey Meatballs with Blueberries & Balsamic	Port Wine Lamb Shanks	Corn, Pinto and Quinoa Enchilada with Vegan Cheese	Salmon Poached In Ginger-Miso Broth
Fri	Steamed Cod Mediterranean Style	South East Asian Beef Ribs and White Radish Stew	Spicy Veggie and Tilapia Soup	Sweet and Spicy Three Cups Chicken
Sat	Smoky Butternut Squash Casserole	Instant Pot Roasted Tandoori Chicken	Butternut, Black Bean & Sweet Potato Chili	Raised Beef Ribs
Sun	Pecan Nut & Pumpkin Pie	Chocolate Chip and Cocoa Pudding	Key Lime Pie	Turmeric-Spiced Peach Compote

Menu For Month 38

	Week 1	Week 2	Week 3	Week 4
Mon	Poached Chicken	Port Wine Lamb Shanks	Turkey & Bean Chili	Irish Lamb Stew with Red
Tue	Moroccan Lemon, Lime and Olive Turkey Thighs	Potato and Tofu Stuffed Chilies	Sweet Honey and Lime Barbecue Chicken	Instant Pot Potato and Tofu Stuffed Chilies
Wen	Clam Chowder	Instant Pot Roasted Tomato Gazpacho	Instant Pot Oatmeal Beef Meatballs	Instant Pot Red Beans With Fruity Punch
Thu	Pork Sausage with Bell Peppers & Basil	Instant Pot Vegan Mushroom Lasagna	Pork Carnitas	Turkey Meatballs with Blueberries & Balsamic
Fri	Linguini with Mixed Mushroom Ragout	Instant Pot Ma Po Tofu	Instant Pot Zucchini Shakshuka	Sour Cream and Greek Yogurt Salmon Dip
Sat	Cream of Leek and Bacon Soup	Sour Cream and Greek Yogurt Salmon Dip	Beef and Rosemary Stew	Sweet and Spicy Soy Roast Chicken
Sun	Turmeric-Spiced Peach	Cassava and Sweet Potatoes Pudding with	Pecan Nut & Pumpkin	Pears Poached In Red Wine

	Week 1	Week 2	Week 3	Week 4
Mon	Poached Chicken	Port Wine Lamb Shanks	Turkey & Bean Chili	Irish Lamb Stew with Red
Tue	Moroccan Lemon, Lime and Olive Turkey Thighs	Potato and Tofu Stuffed Chilies	Sweet Honey and Lime Barbecue Chicken	Instant Pot Potato and Tofu Stuffed Chilies
Wen	Clam Chowder	Instant Pot Roasted Tomato Gazpacho	Instant Pot Oatmeal Beef Meatballs	Instant Pot Red Beans With Fruity Punch
Thu	Pork Sausage with Bell Peppers & Basil	Instant Pot Vegan Mushroom Lasagna	Pork Carnitas	Turkey Meatballs with Blueberries & Balsamic
Fri	Linguini with Mixed Mushroom Ragout	Instant Pot Ma Po Tofu	Instant Pot Zucchini Shakshuka	Sour Cream and Greek Yogurt Salmon Dip
Sat	Cream of Leek and Bacon Soup	Sour Cream and Greek Yogurt Salmon Dip	Beef and Rosemary Stew	Sweet and Spicy Soy Roast Chicken
Sun	Turmeric-Spiced Peach	Cassava and Sweet Potatoes Pudding with	Pecan Nut & Pumpkin	Pears Poached In Red Wine

Menu For Month 38

Full colour pictures

Thank you for enjoying my 1000 days of Instant Pot recipes! It has been a pleasure walking you such variety of dishes form cuisines all around the world.

To get a pdf with all full colour pictures at no extra cost, click on the link below:

http://bit.ly/IPOTBOOKCOLOUR

Made in the USA
Columbia, SC
09 December 2019